HRM Ethics:
Perspectives for
a New Millennium

Linda Gravett, Ph.D., SPHR
Xavier University

Book Activation Key

017 18A861

This key activates your online textbook.
Scratch off gray area above to see your book activation key. If the key is
already visible, then it has been used and is no longer valid. Contact us at
www.atomicdog.com or **800-310-5661 x6** to order your online textbook.

ATOMIcdogPUBLISHING

Cincinnati, Ohio
www.atomicdog.com

Nicole Passo

Dedication

This book is dedicated to my mother, Vivian Kibler, who instilled in me a strong sense of personal values that have served me well in life's challenging and complex times.

When ordering this title, use ISBN 1-931442-58-4.

To order only the online version (Online Study Guide Edition) of this title, use ISBN 1-931442-57-6.

ISBN 1-931442-56-8

Library of Congress Control Number: 2002108523

Printed in the United States of America by Atomic Dog Publishing, 1148 Main Street, Third Floor, Cincinnati, OH 45202.

10 9 8 7 6 5 4 3 2

Contents

Preface vii

Acknowledgments ix

Chapter 1

Introduction 1
Key Terms 1

Chapter 2

What an "Ethical Organization" Looks Like 5
Key Terms 5
Outline 6
2-1 "Scapegoating" 8
2-2 Abdicating Responsibility 8
2-3 Overpromising 8
2-4 "Turf Guarding" 9
2-5 Underachieving 9
2-6 Three Ethics Tests for Individuals 9
  2-6a Test #1: The "Butterflies" Test 10
  2-6b Test #2: The Authority Test 10
  2-6c Test #3: The Public Scrutiny Test 10

Chapter 3

**Ethical Dilemma #1: An Intervention with a Manager
Who Is Related to the CEO** 13
Key Terms 13
Outline 14
3-1 Breakdown by Total 14
3-2 Breakdown by Race and Ethnicity 17
3-3 Breakdown by Gender 24

3-4 Breakdown by Age and Number of Years
   in Human Resources   30
3-5 Breakdown by Organization-Level Characteristics   41
  3-5a Breakdown by Organization Type   41
  3-5b Breakdown by Organization Size   51
Chapter Summary   53
Discussion Questions   53

Chapter 4

**Ethical Dilemma #2: A Supervisor Has HIV and
Is a Gay-Rights Activist—Who Has a Right to Know?   55**

Key Terms   55
Outline   56
4-1 Breakdown by Total   56
4-2 Breakdown by Race and Ethnicity   58
4-3 Breakdown by Gender   62
4-4 Breakdown by Number of Years in Human Resources   65
4-5 Breakdown by Age   69
4-6 Breakdown by Organization Type   73
4-7 Breakdown by Organization Size   76
Chapter Summary   80
Discussion Questions   82

Chapter 5

**Ethical Dilemma #3: To Explore or Not
to Explore a Rumor—That Is the Question   83**

Key Terms   83
Outline   84
5-1 Breakdown by Total   85
5-2 Breakdown by Race and Ethnicity   86
5-3 Breakdown by Gender   87
5-4 Breakdown by the Number of Years in Human Resources and Age   89
5-5 Breakdown by Organization Type   91
5-6 Breakdown by Organization Size   93
Chapter Summary   94
Discussion Questions   95

Chapter 6

**Ethical Dilemma #4: The Boss Wants to Replace Employees with Robots—
Should Human Resources Intervene?   97**

Key Terms   97
Outline   98
6-1 Breakdown by Total   99
6-2 Breakdown by Race and Ethnicity   100
6-3 Breakdown by Number of Years in Human Resources   104
6-4 Breakdown by Age   106

6-5 Breakdown by Gender   109
6-6 Breakdown by Organization Type   111
6-7 Breakdown by Organization Size   113
Chapter Summary   116
Discussion Questions   117

Chapter 7

Ethical Dilemma #5: How Much "Truth" Should Recruiters Disclose to Applicants?   119

Key Terms   119
Outline   120
7-1 Breakdown by Total   120
7-2 Breakdown by Race and Ethnicity   121
7-3 Breakdown by Gender   123
7-4 Breakdown by Number of Years in Human Resources and Age   125
7-5 Breakdown by Organization Type   128
7-6 Breakdown by Organization Size   129
Chapter Summary   131
Discussion Questions   131

Chapter 8

Ethical Dilemma #6: Monitoring Technology for Telecommuters Is Available, But Should It Be Used?   133

Key Terms   133
Outline   134
8-1 Breakdown by Total   136
8-2 Breakdown by Race and Ethnicity   137
8-3 Breakdown by Gender   139
8-4 Breakdown by Number of Years in Human Resources and Age   142
8-5 Breakdown by Organization Type   147
8-6 Breakdown by Organization Size   149
Chapter Summary   152
Discussion Questions   152

Chapter 9

Ethical Dilemma #7: Can Human Resources Allow Self-Directed Teams to *Really* Be Self-Directed?   153

Key Terms   153
Outline   154
9-1 Breakdown by Total   154
9-2 Breakdown by Gender   155
9-3 Breakdown by Race and Ethnicity   158
9-4 Breakdown by Number of Years in Human Resources and Age   162
9-5 Breakdown by Organization Type   168
9-6 Breakdown by Organization Size   171
Chapter Summary   174
Discussion Questions   175

Chapter 10

The Human Resource Professional's Role in Building an Ethical Organization   177

Key Terms   177
Outline   178
10-1 Core Values   178
10-2 Mutual Trust and Respect   179
10-3 Clear Expectations   180
10-4 Open Communications   181
10-5 Ongoing Education   181
10-6 So What Does This Mean to Me—The Human Resource Practitioner?   182

Appendix A: Ethical Dilemmas of 21st Century Human Resource Professionals—Survey of Current Practices   185
Appendix B: Examples of Codes of Ethics   191
Glossary   197
Index   201

Preface

Today Human Resource Management professionals are challenged with ethical dilemmas that were unheard of 20 years ago. Technology has enhanced organizations' productive capacity and ability to monitor employees' work. Advances in technology also pose privacy concerns, such as how much monitoring is appropriate? Illnesses such as HIV and AIDS place individuals—and potentially, coworkers with whom they come in contact—at risk. Shouldn't anyone who might be exposed to this risk be notified of a person's illness? A global economy has thrust the United States into a competitive marketplace unlike any in the previous century, causing organizations to scramble to find and keep both customers and quality employees. The "bottom line" must be vigorously pursued, but should it be pursued at the expense of integrity?

Into the middle of this milieu walks the Human Resource (HR) practitioner.

This book offers an ethical framework for decision making for managers who must make decisions involving people. The results of a survey of over 500 HR professionals in organizations throughout the United States are shared, and differences across age, race, gender, organization type, and organization size are discussed. The survey posed seven real-world ethical dilemmas and asked how respondents would handle each situation in their own organization.

The reader is provided with provocative questions for discussion at the end of most chapters. This book will help readers to become actively involved in establishing a set of guidelines that anchors their ethical decision-making process.

Please note: *HRM Ethics* is available online as well as in print. We don't want you getting lost as you move between the Web and print formats, so we numbered the primary heads and subheads in each chapter the same. For example, the first primary head in Chapter 2 is labeled 2-1, the second primary head in this chapter is labeled 2-2, and so on. The subheads build from the designation of their corresponding primary head: 2-1a, 2-1b, etc.

The numbering system is designed to make moving between the online and print versions as seamless as possible. So if your instructor tells you to read the material in 2-3 and 2-4 for tomorrow's assignment, you'll know that the information appears in Chapter 2 of both the Web and print versions of the text, and you can then choose the best way for you to complete the assignment.

 Finally, next to figure 2-1 in the print version of the text, you will see an icon similar to the one on the left. This icon indicates that this figure in the online version of the text is interactive in a way that applies, illustrates, or reinforces the concept.

Acknowledgments

As a neophyte author, I owe a debt of thanks to many people who helped make this book possible. First and foremost, I'd like to say thank you to Steve Scoble at Atomic Dog Publishing for his advice, patience, and diplomacy.

I'd like to thank the 518 Human Resource practitioners who took their valuable time to complete an ethics survey built around seven ethical dilemmas. The survey results form the heart of the book and helped me understand current thinking in the Human Resource Management field.

Thank you to Troy Bartson from Clopay Corporation, Bill Miller from Cintas, and Steve Browne from CDS Engineers for sharing your organizations' ethics guidelines. Your generosity is appreciated.

Through personal interviews, Alfonso Cornejo and Tina Macon provided me with insights into the Hispanic and African American cultures, which have been incorporated into this book. These perspectives were of tremendous value.

Chapter

1

Introduction

Key Terms

Americans With Disabilities Act
Civil Rights Act
Ethnicity

Human Resource Practitioner
Relativism

A **Human Resource practitioner,** or anyone who serves in a leadership capacity within an organization, is often faced with multiple choices about how to handle ethical dilemmas. Human Resource professionals encounter unique situations because most employee relations issues fall within their scope of responsibility. Laws such as Title VII of the **Civil Rights Act** and **The Americans With Disabilities Act** provide legal guidelines for handling employee relations; however, it is possible to comply with these laws and still not be on solid, ethical ground. In *The Ethics of Excellence,*[1] Price Pritchett says, "sometimes people hide behind laws to do their dirty deeds. You could get away with a lot of ugly stuff without ever being fined or sent to jail."

With the assistance of legal counsel, we can determine the law. We can calculate the bottom-line impact of decisions. However, making the *right* choice when people are involved can be challenging. A complicating issue is that the concept of ethics means different things to different people. This book explores those differences as they relate to age, gender, culture, number of years in Human Resources, organization size, and type of industry.

The field of Human Resource Management has evolved into a strategic, technical, and measurement-oriented area in the past decade. The field will continue to grow in sophistication and complexity as a reflection of the world in the 21st century, presenting difficult ethical dilemmas. For more discussion about how ethics will play an increasingly important role in Human Resource Management, see white papers submitted by Peter Panken and Howard M. Pardue, Ph.D. (http://www.shrm.org/whitepapers/default.asp?page=manage.htm).

Chapter 2 describes what an ethical organization looks like; discusses indicators of a weak ethics system and the resulting damage to productivity and profitability; and explains the Human Resource professional's potential to contribute to the development of an ethical organization.

In a survey of 518 Human Resource professionals in late 2000, seven ethical dilemmas were described to respondents. Survey participants were asked to discuss how they would address these dilemmas in their organizations. Appendix A contains a sample of the survey. Survey results were compiled first across the total population of 518 respondents and then breakouts were compiled based on individual and organizational characteristics. Chapters 3–9 reveal the differences in responses to the seven scenarios across the demographic groups of age, gender, race and **ethnicity,** number of years in Human Resources, and across organizations of different sizes and industries.

---

1. Pritchett, Price. 1999. *The Ethics of Excellence.* Dallas, TX: Pritchett and Associates, Inc., page 6.

The role of Human Resources in organizations is multifaceted. Line managers look to Human Resources as an internal consultant, an advisor with regard to policies that involve employee relations, and an objective enforcer of the organization's rules and regulations. What happens when Human Resources discovers that a manager is engaging in practices that could damage the organization—and that manager is related to the CEO? This situation is addressed in Chapter 3.

This past decade has seen the incidence of HIV and AIDS, and related illnesses occur at alarming rates. Chapter 4 discusses a highly sensitive issue in today's workplace: a first-line supervisor who has been diagnosed as HIV-positive has alerted Human Resources to this fact *and* disclosed that he plans to become a gay-rights activist. Human Resources is faced with the dilemma of preserving the supervisor's privacy while protecting the rights of other employees and the public.

Unions are still viable in many U.S. organizations, and Human Resource professionals become involved in negotiations for a new or continued contract. It is not savvy to put forth one's position immediately and show your hand . . . or is it? What if Human Resources becomes aware of a rumor that, if true, could affect the outcome of the negotiations? Chapter 5 poses a dilemma that suggests a new ethical approach will be necessary in the coming years to successfully bring all parties to a "win-win" agreement.

Over the next decade, technology will continue to move at warp speed. Rapidly changing technology can serve organizations well in terms of improving productivity and, at the same time, present ethical questions managers have not had to face until recently. Robotics is emerging as an optional form of labor in the manufacturing arena. This fact creates dilemmas around retraining and retaining employees who are no longer needed. Chapter 6 covers this scenario. With the increase of employees in the U.S. workforce opting to telecommute, Human Resources is faced with the challenge of managing the productivity of staff that is not physically on site. Questions emerge such as, "Should technology be used to monitor the time people log on to their computers in the morning or to count the number of keystrokes they use?" This scenario is addressed in Chapter 8.

Many organizations have reduced levels of management and developed functional or cross-functional work teams with decision-making authority. The concept behind self-directed work teams is that the team has the authority to make decisions such as hiring and firing team members. What, then, is the responsibility of the Human Resource professional who becomes aware that staffing decisions may be based on team members' personal preferences or personality conflicts within the team? Chapter 9 describes this scenario and poses the question, "How and when should Human Resources intervene?"

This book will address dilemmas that Human Resource practitioners face today and will be facing in the first decade of the new millennium. The scenarios are real—they happened to Human Resource professionals in companies throughout the United States and have been recounted in personal interviews. While no one person has the definitive answer to handling every nuance of ethical dilemmas, Chapter 10 will provide some practical guidelines to follow in order to take an active role in building an organization with a strong, ethical framework. This book will endeavor to convince readers that a sound, ethical foundation results in higher productivity and customer satisfaction and will provide insight into the phrase, "doing the right thing right."

I would like to also say a word about what this book is *not* about. This book does not strive to describe and analyze various ethical frameworks such as relativism. Some excellent work has already been done in this area, and I refer readers who are curious about various ethical philosophies to http://www.pilgrimpress.com; *After Principles, Ethics* by Garrett Barden[2]; *The Morality of Groups: Collective Responsibility, Group-Based Harm, and Corporate Right* by Larry May.[3]

2. Barden, Garrett. 1992. *After Principles, Ethics.* Available at Amazon.com.

3. May, Larry. 1990, January. *The Morality of Groups: Collective Responsibility, Group-Based Harm, and Corporate Right.* Available at Amazon.com.

Chapter

2

What an "Ethical Organization" Looks Like

Key Term

Ethnicity

O u t l i n e

2-1 "Scapegoating"
2-2 Abdicating Responsibility
2-3 Overpromising
2-4 "Turf Guarding"
2-5 Underachieving
2-6 Three Ethics Tests for Individuals
    2-6a Test #1: The "Butterflies" Test
    2-6b Test #2: The Authority Test
    2-6c Test #3: The Public Scrutiny Test

Think of an organization in the United States that you would describe as "ethical." Perhaps Johnson & Johnson, the manufacturers of Tylenol, comes to mind. Remember the Tylenol scare in the early 1980s? Tylenol laced with cyanide was responsible for killing seven people in Chicago, so Johnson & Johnson recalled all the product from the shelves. This was certainly a significant cost to Johnson & Johnson; however, it took the only ethical course of action.

Individuals within an organization can hold and practice core values; however, that does not mean that the organization as a whole is ethical. To lay the foundation for an ethical organization, its leadership must establish, publish, and model the company's core values.

I have enjoyed the opportunity of doing some consulting work with Toyota's Georgetown, Kentucky plant. I am impressed with the fact that its Statement of Core Values is more than just "wallpaper." In 2000, the company provided training for all employees (yes, I said *all* employees), which covered examples of expected, ethical behaviors that support Toyota's Mission, Vision, and Core Values. Consequently, employees are now more thoughtful about decisions they make and what they say to coworkers and customers.

While each organization must establish its own ethical framework, I suggest that two cornerstones must be in place to build an ethical organization: mutual trust and respect. In personal interviews conducted with 100 Human Resource practitioners across the United States in 1999 and 2000, these two characteristics surfaced time and again as critical components of ethical organizations.

In an organization in which respect is a demonstrated value, employees and managers treat each other with dignity and make it known that they care about the work they perform. The organization's leadership fosters initiative and creativity. Individual differences and perspectives are

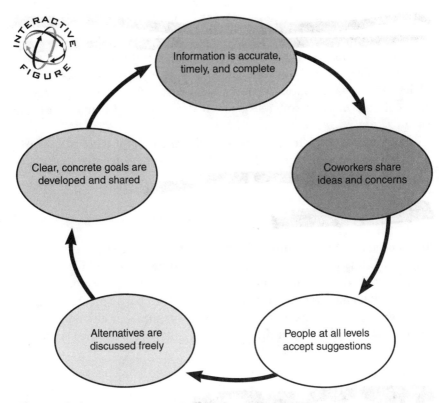

Figure 2-1   Components of ethical organizations.

appreciated and promoted. All employees, regardless of their position, are recognized and rewarded for their contributions (Figure 2-1). In their book titled, *Built on Trust,*[1] Arky Ciancutti and Thomas Steding suggest:

"An environment rich in trust creates an engine for innovation."

I agree: innovation can provide a competitive edge, and Human Resource professionals should proactively foster innovation within their organizations.

Many people subscribe to the belief that a person has to earn respect. I have a different perspective. I believe in affording respect to anyone I meet, automatically. I am here; they are here. Their potential value as a contributing member of society is the same as mine. A person may do

---

1. Ciancutti, Arky, and Steding, Thomas. 2000. *Built on Trust.* Contemporary Books. pg. xiii.

something to lose my respect as time goes by; however, I am willing to operate on a level of mutual respect until and unless that event occurs.

In an organization where trust is prevalent, information is accurate, timely, and complete. Coworkers share their ideas and concerns. People at all levels accept suggestions for ways to improve the work. Alternatives are freely discussed. Clear, concrete goals are developed and shared across the organization.

There are clues within the organizational culture if trust and respect are *not* threads in the cultural fabric. Here are some behaviors that I have observed in organizations with a weak ethics system:

2-1 "Scapegoating"

If "scapegoating" is a common phenomenon in your culture, this is a red flag that failure may not be tolerated and it is necessary to hide mistakes or errors in judgment. When customer complaints occur, perhaps employees blame everyone else or every other department. When goals are not achieved, individuals actively search for someone else on which to lay the blame. In the meantime, it is likely that customer needs are not being met.

2-2 Abdicating Responsibility

When the time comes to make a decision and stand by that decision or action, how do people in the organization respond? If common excuses are, "I am not aware of any problems—I asked Joe to handle that" or "I assigned that to a member of my staff—I don't know what's happening," this is an indicator of abdication behavior. People in an ethical organization accept responsibility for themselves and their direct reports. Period. The focus should be on owning problems, not on the rote response, "It's not my job."

2-3 Overpromising

"This company is the best place to work in the county!" "The promotion path here is extremely fast." "We'll be going public within the year!" Are managers using these kinds of statements frequently without knowing whether they are really true? If the norm is making brash, optimistic statements to achieve a short-term result, this is an indicator of a weak ethics system. In Chapter 7, we will see an example of recruiters who are tempted not to disclose any negative information about their company to applicants. I would rather applicants know "both sides of the story" than leave after a month when they discover things are not quite as rosy as promised.

2-4 "Turf Guarding"

In today's ever-changing marketplace, companies must be highly flexible to meet customer demands. The result is that employees must be prepared to shift gears and learn new skills or serve on various work teams to complete projects. If an organization has employees who hoard information and jealously guard their turf for any reason, productivity may suffer and resentment can build. This behavior is an indicator that people do not trust their knowledge or expertise in someone else's hands . . . or believe their job is in jeopardy if other employees show promise. Employees must be recognized and rewarded for sharing, not hoarding, information.

2-5 Underachieving

Are employees allowed to barely "get by" and still be rewarded with a paycheck and even promotions? Is mediocrity accepted because it is too difficult to fire people who are not really competent? If an organization takes the easy way out and tolerates employees who are negative and only partially productive, long-term success is jeopardized. How many customers and employees must leave before a company holds that one person accountable?

My experience from working with organizations as a consultant for over 10 years is that the organization's leadership plays a significant part in establishing the culture. If an organization deals with its customers, vendors, and employees ethically, the individual leaders have made intentional choices that demonstrate a high level of integrity.

2-6 Three Ethics Tests for Individuals

I believe we should look inwardly first, then to others we respect to test our ethical choices. Lawrence Kohlberg's books and articles about the stages of moral development (see www.bn.com to view a list of his books) offer the theory that people reach a stage in their moral development in which they value the opinions and needs of others. In *The Ethics of*

Excellence,[2] Price Pritchett suggests, "The best bet is to discuss the matter with people whose ethics you admire—those you respect for their honesty, fairness, and integrity."

2-6a Test #1: The "Butterflies" Test

Have you ever felt inwardly that something you were about to do was questionable, but you did it anyway? I'll bet you would like to have that decision back.

Prior to making a decision or engaging in a behavior, some people get "butterflies" in their stomach. This is a physical, involuntary reaction to stressful situations that causes people to take notice of what they are about to say or do. This uncertainty may be precipitated by doubts that a proposed action is the best for all stakeholders. Perhaps there is a concern about the impact of an action on employees or coworkers. This instinct is important and should be trusted. This is a sign that it is necessary to pause and reflect on one's own and the organization's values before acting.

2-6b Test #2: The Authority Test

When someone uses the authority test, he or she thinks about a person whose opinion is highly valued and asks, "What would that person do in a similar situation?" or "What would that person think about how I reacted to this challenge?" The authority can be a mentor, a trusted peer, a teacher, or anyone viewed as competent in the area in question. I think about what my mother would do, and whether she would be proud of me for taking the steps I chose.

2-6c Test #3: The Public Scrutiny Test

People about to make a decision or engage in a behavior that is questionable can ask themselves, "Can I accept public review of this decision or behavior?" What if an article about one's actions would be published in the local newspaper or splashed across the headlines in the evening news? Decisions or actions must be defensible in a public forum. That is not to say that every single person observing the action would agree that it is the right thing to do, but the underlying values that precipitated the action should be clear to observers.

---

2. Pritchett, *The Ethics of Excellence,* page 12.

Human Resource professionals are likely to be challenged daily with issues that present ethical dilemmas. The choices that they make, or guide others to make, may affect the productivity, profitability, and the public image of their organizations. That public image affects their company's ability to recruit employees *and* customers in the future.

In the following chapters, actual scenarios are presented along with survey results from 518 Human Resource professionals across the United States who shared how they would handle the ethical dilemmas in their organizations. At the end of each chapter, questions are posed to you, the reader, about how you would respond to these challenges.

Survey results have been compiled across the entire population of respondents, shown in Table 2-1. Breakouts are analyzed based on both individual and organization characteristics. Individual characteristics pulled out for study are race and **ethnicity**, gender, age, and number of years in Human Resources. Organization characteristics studied are organization type (manufacturing, service, not-for-profit, and public sector) and size.

T A B L E **2-1** Survey Respondents (N = 518)

Category	Number in Each Category/Percentage of Total				
Gender				Male 166 (32%)	Female 352 (68%)
Race/Ethnicity		Caucasian	African American	Asian	Hispanic
		316 (61%)	135 (26%)	41 (8%)	26 (5%)
Age		<30 191 (37%)	31–40 234 (45%)	41–50 60 (12%)	51–60 33 (6%)
Years in HR	<1 89 (17%)	2–3 102 (20%)	4–5 58 (11%)	6–10 176 (34%)	>10 93 (18%)
Organization Type		Mfg 94 (18%)	Svc 197 (38%)	NFP 52 (10%)	PS 175 (34%)
Organization Size	<100 29 (6%)	101–500 73 (14%)	501–1000 159 (31%)	1001–5000 136 (26%)	5001–10,000 121 (23%)

Abbreviations: Mfg = manufacturing
Svc = service
NFP = not-for-profit
PS = public sector

Chapter 3

Ethical Dilemma #1: An Intervention with a Manager Who Is Related to the CEO

Key Terms

Age Discrimination in Employment Act
  (ADEA)
African American
Asian
Caucasian
Eurocentric

Family and Medical Leave Act (FMLA)
Generation Xers
Hispanic
Prima facie

Outline

3-1 Breakdown by Total
3-2 Breakdown by Race and Ethnicity
3-3 Breakdown by Gender
3-4 Breakdown by Age and Number of Years in Human Resources
3-5 Breakdown by Organization-Level Characteristics
    3-5a Breakdown by Organization Type
    3-5b Breakdown by Organization Size
Chapter Summary
Discussion Questions

A highly productive manager in your organization, who was born and raised in the Middle East, finds a reason to reject all females recommended by Human Resources for professional or technical positions in his department. The manager is the CEO's son-in-law. What, if anything, should Human Resources do about this situation?

In this scenario, the Human Resources professional is faced with legal issues related to discrimination based on sex, the manager's need for coaching in the area of recruiting and selection, and an ethical dilemma—the manager is the CEO's son-in-law. Advising managers about interviewing techniques and discussing Title VII of the Civil Rights Act with regard to discrimination are activities that Human Resource professionals engage in on a frequent basis. The sensitive issue here is the fact that anyone who approaches the manager also risks offending the CEO—who is close to the person who is in a position to control employment.

The manager may not be acting in the best interests of the company because he is establishing a viable case for discrimination based on sex. On the other hand, this manager may have some protection from criticism or interference because of his relationship to the CEO. If Human Resources appears to question the manager's choices or make an effort to coach him, the manager could be angered by the perceived interference with his job.

3-1 Breakdown by Total

Table 3-1 shows the compilation of survey results for ethical dilemma 1. Over half (56%) of the respondents report that they would ignore the fact that the manager is the CEO's son-in-law and would proceed as if he were any other manager. I was surprised to find that the remaining respondents (44%) avoided this issue altogether and made no comment about the familial relationship.

T A B L E **3-1**   **Breakdown by Total**

Ignore relationship/proceed as normal	56%
No comment about relationship	44%
Don't jump to conclusions about sexism	47%
Take appropriate steps in prima facie case for sexism is discovered	36%
Educate and counsel the manager	25%
Go directly to the CEO	18%

Just under half of the respondents suggest that Human Resources should not automatically jump to the conclusion that the manager does not want women in professional or technical positions in his department. Many in this group caution that making an assumption such as, "A person from the Middle East does not approve of women in the workplace" unfairly stereotypes the manager. The majority of respondents in this category recommend that an HR representative meet with the manager, explain that his actions may result in legal problems for the organization, and attempt to discern whether he is rejecting women simply because of gender bias. Another common suggestion among this group is that the manager's interview notes from previous hires be reviewed to search for patterns or trends that indicate his hiring criteria.

Over one-third of the respondents indicate they would proactively take further steps after reviewing the manager's interview notes *if* there appears to be a **prima facie** case for discrimination based on sex. A small percentage of respondents (7%) would proactively respond to an apparent case of sex discrimination to avoid being personally named in potential lawsuits for condoning discriminatory acts. Because of recent court cases allowing employees to name managers in lawsuits, I would have expected more people to be in this category! (See SHRM white paper titled, *Personal Liability of Human Resource Professionals in Employment Litigation*, by Scott Fredericksen, January 1997, at http://www.shrm.org/whitepapers/default.asp?page=manage.htm.)

One-fourth of the respondents indicate they would attempt to educate and counsel the manager regardless of whether he seems to be discriminating based on sex. The counseling would address the cultural differences between the manager's native country and those of the United States with regard to women in the workplace. Another 13% suggest that the manager be required to attend diversity training, and 3% believe that the Human Resources professional should recognize this experience as an indicator that HR must become educated about cultural diversity. With this low response rate in support of cultural awareness for our profession,

I feel compelled at this point to encourage HR professionals to examine their understanding of the many cultural perspectives represented in the workforce. The **Eurocentric** perspective will not always be persuasive in today's workplace.   *European Caucasion*

Only a small percentage of respondents recommend building a partnership with the manager and coaching him in ways to establish criteria for future positions. This group also believes that HR should review the manager's interview notes prior to any job offers he made to ensure that his selections were based on objective criteria. Another 8% of respondents believe it is necessary to sit in on future interviews with the manager to determine if he requires training in interview techniques.

The possibility that HR's attempts at educating the manager and convincing him to use objective selection criteria could fail is addressed by a small percentage of respondents (18%). This group would go directly to the CEO and advise of the potential for legal liability if the manager is not willing to change his hiring methods. Remember that 56% of the respondents assert that the manager's relationship to the CEO should not be a factor in HR's response. A considerably smaller number is actually willing to take the issue directly to the CEO. A small percentage would discuss the situation with senior managers and attempt to garner their support to change the manager's hiring methods.

Within the group of 92 respondents who would go directly to the CEO, 21% indicate they would resign if the CEO is unwilling to support them by requiring the manager to hire qualified women. These respondents said they could not work in an organization that condones discrimination of any kind. Another 41% within this group suggest that the HR person should document steps taken to minimize discrimination and should maintain that documentation at home for safekeeping. I have to wonder about the organizations they come from. Is self-protection a survival strategy they have had to learn? One-fourth of this group would verbally go on record with the CEO regarding their disapproval of the manager's hiring practices, and just 13% would continue to attempt to change the manager's hiring criteria.

A small percentage of respondents suggest that the hiring practices of all departments within the organization be reviewed to determine if there is evidence of discrimination in other areas. This group also recommends company-wide training on hiring and selection procedures for all hiring managers. I know this may seem like punishing the many for the sins of the few; however, I agree that a company needs to explore organization-

Management Authority   Legal Vulnerability

Figure 3-1   Balance between management control and the law.

wide policies and procedures periodically to ensure fairness and legal compliance are consistent practices (Figure 3-1).

3-2 Breakdown by Race and Ethnicity

Let me share with you the breakdown across all 518 respondents as a whole (Table 3-2) and then look at some interesting differences across different racial groups (Table 3-2a–n). Within the response set, **Caucasians** comprise the largest percentage (61%), followed by **African Americans** (26%), **Asians** (8%), and **Hispanics** (5%).

TABLE **3-2**   **Breakdown by Race and Ethnicity**

Category	Percentage	Number
Caucasian	61%	316
African American	26%	135
Asian	8%	41
Hispanic	5%	26
	100%	518

TABLE **3-2a**

Disregard the fact that the manager is related to the CEO. (291)

Category	Number	% of 291	% of Group
Caucasian	126	43	40
African American	110	38	81
Asian	12	4	29
Hispanic	9	3	35

TABLE **3-2b**

No comment was made regarding the manager's relationship to the CEO. (227)

Category	Number	% of 227	% of Group
Caucasian	190	84	60
African American	25	11	19
Asian	29	13	71
Hispanic	17	7	65

TABLE **3-2c**

Don't jump to the conclusion that the manager does not want to hire women—have a meeting with him and discuss his interview notes. (242)

Category	Number	% of 242	% of Group
Caucasian	213	88	67
African American	23	10	17
Asian	4	2	10
Hispanic	2	1	8

TABLE **3-2d**

Proactively respond to the situation if there is a prima facie case for discrimination based on sex. (189)

Category	Number	% of 189	% of Group
Caucasian	106	56	33.5
African American	62	33	46
Asian	13	7	32
Hispanic	8	4	31

T A B L E **3-2e**

Proactively respond to the situation because you do not want to be sued for helping the manager discriminate based on sex. (36)

Category	Number	% of 36	% of Group
Caucasian	14	39	4
African American	10	28	7
Asian	7	19	17
Hispanic	5	14	19

T A B L E **3-2f**

Discuss the implications of the situation with the manager, even if you do not believe discrimination is occurring; attempt to counsel and educate the manager about cultural differences between the United States and his native country. (130)

Category	Number	% of 130	% of Group
Caucasian	47	36	15
African American	52	40	39
Asian	15	12	37
Hispanic	16	12	62

T A B L E **3-2g**

Outline together criteria for jobs that become available and encourage the manager to focus on these criteria. Review interview notes prior to hiring to ensure this happens. (35)

Category	Number	% of 35	% of Group
Caucasian	13	37	4
African American	10	29	7
Asian	6	17	15
Hispanic	6	17	23

T A B L E **3-2h**

Have the manager attend diversity training. (67)

Category	Number	% of 67	% of Group
Caucasian	23	34	7
African American	28	42	21
Asian	13	19	32
Hispanic	3	4	11.5

T A B L E **3-2i**

Sit in on future interviews with the manager so you can determine if he needs coaching on interview practices. (44)

Category	Number	% of 44	% of Group
Caucasian	26	59	8
African American	17	39	13
Asian	0	0	0
Hispanic	2	4.5	8

T A B L E **3-2j**

Discuss the situation and potential damage to the company with senior management. Attempt to get their support about appropriate hiring practices from now on. (34)

Category	Number	% of 34	% of Group
Caucasian	19	56	6
African American	7	21	5
Asian	5	15	12
Hispanic	3	9	11.5

T A B L E **3-2k**

If the manager does not change, go to the CEO and discuss the potential Title VII impact and why it is important to have objective hiring criteria. (92)

Category	Number	% of 92	% of Group
Caucasian	37	40	12
African American	40	43	30
Asian	10	12	24
Hispanic	5	5	19

T A B L E **3-2l**

If the CEO does not respond by supporting Human Resources, the HR person should quit. (19)

Category	Number	% of 19	% of Group
Caucasian	7	39	2
African American	10	53	7
Asian	0	0	0
Hispanic	2	10.5	8

T A B L E **3-2l** (continued)

The HR person should document steps taken and keep a copy of documentation at home. (38)

Category	Number	% of 38	% of Group
Caucasian	12	32	4
African American	16	42	12
Asian	4	10.5	10
Hispanic	6	16	23

Verbally go on record with the CEO that you disapprove of the manager's hiring practices. (23)

Category	Number	% of 23	% of Group
Caucasian	7	30	2
African American	10	43	7
Asian	2	9	5
Hispanic	4	17	15

Continue to try to change the manager's hiring practices. (12)

Category	Number	% of 12	% of Group
Caucasian	8	67	2.5
African American	3	25	2
Asian	0	0	0
Hispanic	1	8	4

T A B L E **3-2m**

Review other units within the company to determine if adverse impact of any kind is taking place. If it is, conduct training on hiring and selection. (39)

Category	Number	% of 39	% of Group
Caucasian	20	51	6
African American	7	18	5
Asian	8	21	19.5
Hispanic	4	10	15

T A B L E **3-2n**

The HR person should take this situation as a clue that HR must become educated about cultural differences. (14)

Category	Number	% of 14	% of Group
Caucasian	3	1	1
African American	6	43	4
Asian	2	14	5
Hispanic	3	21	11.5

A very high percentage of African Americans assert that Human Resources should ignore the fact that the manager with questionable hiring practices is related to the CEO. Less than half of the Caucasian respondents, only 35% of Hispanics, and 29% of Asians make this statement. Typical of the comments by African American respondents are, "It's important to stand up for what is right, even if the CEO may ultimately disagree" and, "There are qualified people not being considered for jobs they can potentially do, and that must be stopped." African American responses to this scenario show a high level of empathy toward people who are discounted because of an immutable characteristic.

Only 92 of our respondents say they would actually try to meet with the CEO if the manager refuses to rethink his hiring methodology. Almost one-third (30%) of African Americans would take this approach, followed by 24% of Asian respondents. Regardless of race, most respondents in this group would position the discussion with the CEO around potential Title VII discrimination based on gender and try to impress upon the CEO how expensive litigation in this area could be for the organization. I have found this approach useful in getting the CEO's attention: talk about the cost of the problem first, then discuss potential solutions.

I had the opportunity to live in Japan for 3 years and to work for 4 years with an international manufacturing company headquartered in the United States that has Japanese representatives. I learned through these experiences that a facet of Japanese culture is respect for position within an organization. If a person is not at the same rank as the CEO, he or she does not even consider going directly to that person to broach a suggestion. The expectation is that one deals directly with a person on the same level within the hierarchy. Within this culture, a Human Resources person would not contemplate meeting directly with the CEO, and would only meet with the hiring manager if this person were on the same organizational level as Human Resources.

A high percentage (96%) of the Asian response set is Japanese. Research indicates that Japanese are very focused on the good of the organization as opposed to the elevation of individuals (www.cic.sfu.ca/). On the other hand, according to Japanese business protocol (see www.asiasource.org), one's exact position in the company and association to a known person are very important. This may account for the surprisingly low percentage of Asian respondents who would not go directly to the CEO and advise of activities that could potentially damage the organization.

Many Asian respondents indicate that HR should take an indirect approach toward changing the manager's hiring practices. Almost one-third of the Asian respondents recommend that the manager be sent to diversity training in the hope that this experience would change his perspective on hiring women. Another 12% of Asian respondents would seek out the support of senior managers, recognizing their influence in changing someone related to the CEO as being greater than their own.

An interesting newsletter article on an Asian Web site (www.goldsea.com) titled "When Worlds Near-Miss," asserts that the U.S.-born or second-generation Asians learned from their parents to be "tolerant and patient with the foibles of others." The article suggests that this approach is not productive in the current U.S. workplace because forbearance will be taken as weakness, and that people of Asian heritage must learn to confront individuals with whom they disagree.

A high percentage (89%) of the Hispanic response set is from Latin America. My discussions with Hispanic consultants in the field of organizational development reveal that Latin Americans lag behind the United States with regard to gender equity in the workplace. Hispanics in Human Resource roles in the United States who come from this background may want to politely tell line managers that they are not meeting the expectations for fair hiring standards by providing diversity training or coaching on setting objective hiring criteria. A high percentage of Hispanic respondents suggests that a Human Resources representative discuss with the manager the cultural differences between the United States and the Middle East with regard to the role of women in the workplace.

Only 19 out of the 518 respondents to the survey say that they would quit if the CEO does not support Human Resources, and 10 of these people are African American. A common theme is that they do not want to work for a company that condones inequitable treatment of any segment of the workforce. This group's empathy for others who have been treated badly is high.

Let us contrast these findings with how Caucasian respondents would handle this ethical dilemma. A majority of Caucasian respondents (67%) caution that Human Resources should not jump to the conclusion that the hiring manager does not want to hire women in technical and professional positions. This group suggests that a meeting be held with the manager to ascertain if he does indeed have gender bias or if legitimate barriers exist, such as a shortage of qualified women with the required competencies in the labor pool.

Just over one-third (33.5%) of Caucasians suggest that Human Resources should investigate why the manager is not hiring women for specific positions and proactively intervene *if* there is a prima facie case of discrimination based on sex. The impetus behind these respondents' suggested course of action is the law as opposed to any other factor. Over half (60%) of the Caucasian respondents do not address the issue of the manager's relationship to the CEO in providing an answer to this dilemma.

These results lead to the conclusion that approaches to the first ethical dilemma differ across racial and ethnic groups. A large number of African American respondents are empathic toward a qualified segment of the workforce that is (perhaps) being discounted for factors not related to the job. Many Asian respondents are torn between the manager's proximity to the CEO and their desire to protect the interests of the organization, so they recommend indirect action toward changing the manager's practices. Hispanic respondents have the most variety in terms of interventions suggested to solve this dilemma, from documenting steps taken to minimize discrimination to going on record with the CEO that they disapprove of the manager's hiring practices. A common theme across comments from Hispanics is the expectation that senior leaders should act honestly and ethically and should stand behind those (such as Human Resources) who are authorized to speak on behalf of the organization. To this group of respondents, a CEO who fails to support the Human Resources professional is committing a serious breach of faith and is placing the Human Resources person in an untenable situation.

3-3 Breakdown by Gender

Table 3-3 shows a breakdown of respondents by gender.

TABLE **3-3**   **Breakdown by Gender**

M = 166 (32%)	F = 352 (68%)

TABLE **3-3a**

Disregard the fact that the manager is related to the CEO. (261)

Group	Number	% of 261	% of Group
Male	76	29	46
Female	185	71	53

TABLE **3-3b**

No comment was made about manager's relationship to CEO. (257).

Group	Number	% of 257	% of Group
Male	90	35	54
Female	167	65	47

TABLE **3-3c**

Don't jump to the conclusion that the manager does not want to hire women—have a meeting with him and discuss his interview notes. (242)

Group	Number	% of 242	% of Group
Male	118	49	71
Female	124	51	35

TABLE **3-3d**

Proactively respond to the situation if there is a prima facie case for discrimination based on sex. (189)

Group	Number	% of 189	% of Group
Male	92	49	71
Female	97	51	28

TABLE **3-3e**

Proactively respond to the situation because you do not want to be sued for helping the manager discriminate based on sex. (36)

Group	Number	% of 36	% of Group
Male	20	48	12
Female	16	44	4.5

T A B L E **3-3f**

Discuss the implications of the situation with the manager, even if you do not believe discrimination is occurring; attempt to educate/counsel the manager about cultural differences between the United States and his native country. (130)

Group	Number	% of 130	% of Group
Male	63	48	40
Female	67	52	19

T A B L E **3-3g**

Outline together criteria for jobs that become available and encourage the manager to focus on these criteria. Review his interview notes prior to hiring to ensure objectivity. (35)

Group	Number	% of 35	% of Group
Male	12	34	7
Female	23	66	6.5

T A B L E **3-3h**

Have the manager attend diversity training. (67)

Group	Number	% of 67	% of Group
Male	32	48	19
Female	35	52	10

T A B L E **3-3i**

Sit in on future interviews with the manager so you can determine if he needs coaching on interview practices. (44)

Group	Number	% of 44	% of Group
Male	14	32	8
Female	30	68	8.5

TABLE **3-3j**

Discuss the situation and potential damage to the company with senior management. Attempt to gain their support about appropriate hiring practices from now on. (34)

Group	Number	% of 34	% of Group
Male	18	53	29.5
Female	16	47	4.5

TABLE **3-3k**

If the manager does not change, go to the CEO and discuss the potential Title VII impact and why it is important to use objective hiring criteria. (92)

Group	Number	% of 92	% of Group
Male	49	53	29.5
Female	43	47	12

TABLE **3-3l**

If the CEO does not respond by supporting HR, the HR person should quit. (19)

Group	Number	% of 19	% of Group
Male	8	42	5
Female	11	58	3

The HR person should document steps taken and keep a copy of documentation at home. (38)

Group	Number	% of 38	% of Group
Male	21	55	13
Female	17	45	5

Verbally go on record with the CEO that you disapprove of the manager's hiring practices. (23)

Group	Number	% of 23	% of Group
Male	12	52	7
Female	11	45	3

TABLE **3-3l** (continued)

Continue to try to change the manager's hiring practices. (12)

Group	Number	% of 12	% of Group
Male	8	67	5
Female	4	33	1

TABLE **3-3m**

Review other units within the company to determine if adverse impact of any kind is taking place. If yes, conduct training on hiring and selection. (39)

Group	Number	% of 39	% of Group
Male	12	31	7
Female	27	69	8

TABLE **3-3n**

The HR person should take this situation as a clue that HR must become educated about cultural differences. (14)

Group	Number	% of 14	% of Group
Male	8	57	5
Female	6	43	2

Female respondents comprise the larger of the two groups (68%). I expected two distinctly different outlooks between male and female respondents because the gender being (potentially) rejected simply because of sex is women, and there are indeed differences in the approach recommended by men and women.

Seventy-one percent of men caution that Human Resources should not jump to the conclusion that the manager is purposely discriminating against female applicants. A common theme across this group of male respondents is that there may be any number of reasons why the manager is hiring men only for technical and professional positions, and only one of those reasons may be because of gender bias. By contrast, only 51% of the female respondents provide this same caution. The inference we draw from a fact pattern can definitely be different, then, depending on our gender, perhaps in part because of dissimilar workplace experiences that affect our conclusions.

Over half of the male respondents say they would proactively respond by intervening in some way *if* investigation reveals a prima facie case for discrimination based on sex. Only 28% of the female respondents provide this same response. Women in the response group are more likely to intervene regardless of whether there is a potential lawsuit. A higher percentage of male respondents (40%) than female respondents (19%) recommend counseling the manager about the cultural differences between the Middle East and the United States. I am surprised by this, based on my own experiences in the workplace. In *Swim With the Dolphins*,[1] Glaser and Smalley assert that their research indicates that women focus more on interaction skills such as coaching and counseling more than do men. Deborah Sheppard, in an article for *Gendering and Organizational Analysis*,[2] also suggests that women try to build relationships and are "more humanistic."

More men than women suggest that Human Resources should proactively respond to the situation because there is a danger of being personally sued for condoning the manager's discriminatory practices. This response is undoubtedly reflective of the litigious society in which we live in the United States and, if anything, I would have expected a larger group to offer this comment.

A higher percentage of male respondents than female respondents assert that the manager's relationship to the CEO should be disregarded when deciding upon the appropriate action. A common response across male respondents is, "If the manager is causing potential harm to the company, his actions reflect badly on all men." A typical response across female respondents is, "The company won't be able to find applicants for future positions if the company gets the reputation of being biased against women."

Almost 30% of the male respondents recommend that Human Resources attempt to solicit the support of senior managers within the company, as compared to just 4.5% of the female respondents! A higher percentage of male respondents than female respondents would go directly to the CEO to discuss potential Title VII implications. Male respondents' comments center on talking to the CEO "man to man" about the company's potential legal liability. The female respondents more often

---

1. Glaser, Connie and Smalley, Barbara. 1995. *Swim With the Dolphins*. New York: Warner Books, pages 108–109.

2. Sheppard, Deborah. 1992. "Women Managers' Perceptions of Gender and Organizational Life." *Gendering and Organizational Analysis*, Albert J. Mills and Peter Tancred, eds. Newbury Park, CA: Sage Publications, pages 160–161.

suggest an indirect means to change the manager's questionable hiring practices.

This finding supports research by Glaser and Smalley in *Swim With the Dolphins*.[3] They find that women use their sense of humor to motivate and influence others, while men more often engage in rhetoric that "targets the weak, and typically focuses on what one of us did."

You might recall that 19 respondents in the overall response set indicate they would resign if the CEO does not support Human Resources by sanctioning the offending manager. Eleven of the 19 are women and 8 are men.

Thirty-eight respondents caution that the HR professional should document steps taken to change the manager's hiring practices and keep that documentation at home. The majority of this group is male. A slim majority of respondents who would verbally go on record with the CEO with disapproval of the manager's hiring methods is also male. A common theme among these men in their responses is that the workplace is very competitive and it is necessary to protect yourself and your position at all times. As I've worked with men for 20-plus years I have spent in the workplace, I certainly hear more men talk in terms of competition and sports analogies than women, so I am not at all surprised by the comments in the surveys.

There is a very small difference between men and women in some of the suggested approaches. Virtually the same percentage of the male response set and the female response set suggest these interventions:

- Working with the manager to outline criteria for jobs that become available to ensure that the manager understands how to be objective;
- Sitting in on future interviews with the manager to determine if he requires coaching on interview practices;
- Resigning if the CEO does not support Human Resources in changing the manager's hiring practices; and
- Reviewing other units within the company to determine if adverse impact of any kind is taking place.

3-4 Breakdown by Age and Number of Years in Human Resources

Because the age of respondents is closely correlated with the number years in Human Resources, these two breakouts are discussed together.

---

3. Glaser and Smalley, *Swim With the Dolphins*, page 167.

Responses by age are shown in Table 3-4 and responses by years in Human Resources are indicated in Table 3-5.

T A B L E **3-4** Breakdown by Age

Age	Number	% of 518
< 30	191	37
31–40	234	45
41–50	60	12
51–60	33	6
	518	100

T A B L E **3-4a**

Disregard the fact that the manager is related to the CEO. (291)

Age	Number	% of 291	% of Group
< 30	141	48	74
31–40	106	36	45
41–50	29	10	48
51–60	15	5	45

T A B L E **3-4b**

No comment was made about the manager's relationship to the CEO. (227)

Age	Number	% of 227	% of Group
< 30	50	22	11.5
31–40	128	56	24
41–50	31	14	23
51–60	18	8	24

T A B L E **3-4c**

Don't jump to the conclusion that the manager does not want to hire women—have a meeting with him and discuss his interview notes. (242)

Age	Number	% of 242	% of Group
< 30	20	8	10
31–40	163	67	70
41–50	41	17	68
51–60	18	7	54.5

T A B L E **3-4d**

Proactively respond to the situation if there is a prima facie case for discrimination based on sex. (189)

Age	Number	% of 189	% of Group
< 30	87	46	45.5
31–40	66	35	28
41–50	19	10	32
51–60	17	9	51.5

T A B L E **3-4e**

Proactively respond to the situation because you do not want to be sued for helping the manager discriminate based on sex. (36)

Age	Number	% of 36	% of Group
< 30	6	17	3
31–40	23	64	10
41–50	2	6	3
51–60	5	14	15

T A B L E **3-4f**

Discuss the implications of the situation with the manager, even if you do not believe discrimination is occurring; attempt to counsel the manager about cultural differences between the United States and his native country. (130)

Age	Number	% of 130	% of Group
< 30	46	35	24
31–40	46	35	20
41–50	18	14	30
51–60	20	15	61

T A B L E **3-4g**

Outline together criteria for jobs that become available and encourage the manager to focus on these criteria. Review interview notes prior to hiring to ensure objectivity. (35)

Age	Number	% of 35	% of Group
< 30	9	26	5
31–40	14	40	6
41–50	7	20	12
51–60	5	14	15

T A B L E **3-4h**

Have the manager attend diversity training. (67)

Age	Number	% of 67	% of Group
< 30	58	87	30
31–40	5	7	2
41–50	2	3	3
51–60	1	1	3

T A B L E **3-4i**

Sit in on future interviews with the manager so you can determine if he needs coaching on interview practices. (44)

Age	Number	% of 44	% of Group
< 30	15	34	8
31–40	20	45	8.5
41–50	6	14	10
51–60	3	7	9

T A B L E **3-4j**

Discuss the situation and potential damage to the company with senior management. Attempt to get their support about appropriate hiring practices from now on. (34)

Age	Number	% of 34	% of Group
< 30	0	0	0
31–40	21	62	9
41–50	6	18	10
51–60	7	21	21

T A B L E **3-4k**

If the manager does not change, go to the CEO and discuss the potential Title VII impact and why it is important to have objective hiring criteria. (92)

Age	Number	% of 92	% of Group
< 30	40	43	21
31–40	31	34	13
41–50	16	17	27
51–60	5	5	15

TABLE **3-4l**

If the CEO does not respond by supporting Human Resources, the Human Resources person must quit. (19)

Age	Number	% of 19	% of Group
< 30	11	58	6
31–40	8	42	3
41–50	0	0	0
51–60	0	0	0

The HR person should document steps taken and keep a copy of documentation at home. (38)

Age	Number	% of 38	% of Group
< 30	4	11	2
31–40	26	68	11
41–50	7	18	12
51–60	1	3	3

Verbally go on record with the CEO that you disapprove of the manager's hiring practices. (23)

Age	Number	% of 23	% of Group
< 30	6	26	3
31–40	8	35	3
41–50	6	26	10
51–60	3	13	9

Continue to try to change the manager's hiring practices. (12)

Age	Number	% of 12	% of Group
< 30	8	67	4
31–40	3	25	1
41–50	1	8	2
51–60	0	0	0

TABLE **3-4m**

Review other units within the company to determine if adverse impact of any kind is taking place. If yes, conduct training on hiring and selection. (39)

Age	Number	% of 39	% of Group
< 30	13	33	7
31–40	15	38	6
41–50	3	8	5
51–60	8	21	24

TABLE **3-4n**

The HR person should take this situation as a clue that HR must become educated about cultural differences. (14)

Age	Number	% of 14	% of Group
< 30	0	0	0
31–40	12	86	5
41–50	0	0	0
51–60	2	14	6

TABLE **3-5a** **Breakdown by Number of Years in Human Resources**

Disregard the fact that the manager is related to the CEO. (291)

Tenure	Number	% of 291	% of Group
0–1	57	20	64
2–3	84	29	82
4–5	39	13	67
6–10	67	23	38
> 10	44	15	47

TABLE **3-5b**

No comment was made about the manager's relationship to the CEO. (227)

Tenure	Number	% of 227	% of Group
0–1	32	14	36
2–3	18	8	18
4–5	19	8	33
6–10	109	48	62
> 10	49	22	53

TABLE **3-5c**

Don't jump to the conclusion that the manager does not want to hire women in these positions. Have a meeting with him, discuss his interview notes, then investigate why he is rejecting women. (242)

Tenure	Number	% of 242	% of Group
0–1	5	2	6
2–3	15	6	15

T A B L E **3-5c** (continued)

Tenure	Number	% of 242	% of Group
4–5	42	17	72
6–10	121	50	69
> 10	59	24	63

T A B L E **3-5d**

Proactively respond to the situation if there is a prima facie case for discrimination based on sex. (189)

Tenure	Number	% of 189	% of Group
0–1	39	21	44
2–3	48	25	47
4–5	23	12	40
6–10	43	23	24
> 10	36	19	39

T A B L E **3-5e**

Proactively respond to the situation because you do not want to be sued for helping the manager discriminate based on sex. (36)

Tenure	Number	% of 36	% of Group
0–1	0	0	0
2–3	6	17	6
4–5	13	36	22
6–10	10	28	6
> 10	7	19	7.5

T A B L E **3-5f**

Discuss the implications of the situation with the manager, even if you do not believe there is discrimination occurring; attempt to educate and counsel the manager about cultural differences between the United States and his native country. (130)

Tenure	Number	% of 130	% of Group
0–1	25	29	28
2–3	21	16	20.5
4–5	19	15	33
6–10	27	21	15
> 10	38	29	41

TABLE **3-5g**

Outline together criteria for jobs that become available and encourage the manager to focus on these criteria. Review his interview notes prior to hiring and determine if the manager has made his recommendation based on the objective criteria. (35)

Tenure	Number	% of 35	% of Group
0–1	3	9	3
2–3	6	17	6
4–5	0	0	0
6–10	14	40	8
> 10	12	34	13

TABLE **3-5h**

Have the manager attend diversity training. (67)

Tenure	Number	% of 67	% of Group
0–1	31	46	35
2–3	28	42	27
4–5	5	7	9
6–10	0	0	0
> 10	3	4	3

TABLE **3-5i**

Sit in on future interviews with the manager so you can determine if he needs coaching on interview practices. (44)

Tenure	Number	% of 44	% of Group
0–1	6	14	7
2–3	9	20	9
4–5	5	11	9
6–10	15	34	8.5
> 10	9	20	10

TABLE **3-5j**

Discuss the situation and potential damage to the company with senior management. Attempt to get their support about appropriate hiring practices from now on. (34)

Tenure	Number	% of 34	% of Group
0–1	0	0	0
2–3	0	0	0
4–5	12	35	21

T A B L E **3-5j** (continued)

Tenure	Number	% of 34	% of Group
6–10	9	26	5
> 10	13	38	14

T A B L E **3-5k**

If the manager does not change, go to the CEO and discuss the potential Title VII impact and why it is important to use objective hiring criteria. (92)

Tenure	Number	% of 92	% of Group
0–1	21	23	24
2–3	19	21	19
4–5	12	13	21
6–10	19	21	11
> 10	21	23	23

T A B L E **3-5l**

If the CEO does not respond by supporting HR, the HR person must quit. (19)

Tenure	Number	% of 19	% of Group
0–1	6	32	7
2–3	5	26	5
4–5	6	32	10
6–10	2	11	1
> 10	0	0	0

The person should document steps taken and keep a copy of documentation at home. (38)

Tenure	Number	% of 38	% of Group
0–1	1	3	1
2–3	3	8	3
4–5	18	47	31
6–10	8	21	4.5
> 10	8	21	9

Verbally go on record with the CEO that you disapprove of the manager's hiring practices. (23)

Tenure	Number	% of 23	% of Group
0–1	2	9	2
2–3	4	17	4
4–5	1	4	2
6–10	7	30	4
> 10	9	39	10

T A B L E **3-5l** (continued)

Continue trying to change the manager's hiring practices. (12)

Tenure	Number	% of 12	% of Group
0–1	5	42	6
2–3	3	25	3
4–5	0	0	0
6–10	3	25	2
> 10	1	8	1

T A B L E **3-5m**

Review other units within the company to determine if adverse impact of any kind is taking place. If the answer is yes, conduct training on hiring and selection. (39)

Tenure	Number	% of 39	% of Group
0–1	6	15	7
2–3	7	18	7
4–5	7	18	12
6–10	8	21	4.5
> 10	11	28	12

T A B L E **3-5n**

The HR person should take this situation as an indictor that HR must become educated about cultural differences. (14)

Tenure	Number	% of 14	% of Group
0–1	0	0	0
2–3	0	0	0
4–5	3	21	5
6–10	9	64	5
> 10	2	14	2

The largest group represented in the total population is the group with 6 to 10 years of experience in Human Resources (176 respondents). The largest segment by age group is the group between 31–40 (234 respondents).

One significant difference in comments made across age groups is that the two youngest groups, under age 30 and between 31–40, are more concerned about public relations and the company's reputation. The concern these two groups express more than other age groups is that the company's ability to recruit and retain a quality workforce may be affected if the company gains a reputation for discriminating against women. **Generation Xers,** typically considered to be people born between 1965 and 1976, are very conscious of their employer's reputation and integrity (www.emagazine.com/september-october_1999).

Almost three-fourths of the under-30 respondents believe Human Resources should disregard the fact that the manager is related to the CEO when deciding how to handle this dilemma. This finding tracks with research by Zemke, Raines, and Filipczak, in *Generations At Work,*[4] that suggests Generation Xers do not respect others solely because of their title or position.

The younger, less experienced Human Resource respondents indicate the need to respond to this situation proactively if there appears to be a prima facie case for discrimination. HR professionals who have recently completed college programs exposing them to protective labor laws are likely to be very conscious of legal liability, so this is not a surprising finding.

The older, more experienced Human Resource respondents advise not to jump to the conclusion that the manager is purposely rejecting all female applicants. Experience seems to dictate the need for investigation and caution before taking action.

An interesting finding is that the youngest and the oldest respondents are the two groups that suggest the need for educating the manager about discrimination based on sex and the cultural differences between his native country and the United States with regard to women in the workplace. However, the focus of suggestions from the younger respondents is more often on cultural diversity and the focus of suggestions from older respondents is more often on potential Title VII impact.

Less than 25% of the respondents in each of two categories—those with fewer than 1 year and those with over 10 years of Human Resources experience—are willing to set up a meeting with the CEO to discuss legal liability. Younger Human Resources staff have theoretically more chance of securing other employment if they anger the CEO, so I would have expected a higher number in this group to show a willingness to attempt to change a system that could damage the company.

Almost one-third of respondents with 4 to 5 years' experience in Human Resources indicate they would document steps taken to minimize discrimination and keep a record of these steps at home. It is unfortunate that one does not have to be in the field for many years to come to the conclusion that this kind of protective action is necessary.

---

4. Zemke, R., Raines, C., and Filipczak, B. 2000. *Generations At Work.* New York: AMACOM, page 248.

3-5 Breakdown by Organization-Level Characteristics

A breakdown by two organization-level characteristics is provided in Tables 3-6 and 3-7. The compilation in Table 3-6 is by organization type: manufacturing, service, not for profit, or public sector. The compilation in Table 3-7 is by number of employees in one of five categories: 0–100; 101–500; 501–1,000; 1,001–5,000; and 5,001–10,000.

3-5a Breakdown by Organization Type

T A B L E **3-6**   Breakdown by Organization Type

Type	Number	% of 518
Mfg	94	(18)
Svc	197	(38)
NFP	52	(10)
PS	175	(34)

T A B L E **3-6a**

Disregard the fact that the manager is related to the CEO. (291)

Type	Number	% of 291	% of Group
Mfg	62	21	66
Svc	99	34	50
NFP	37	13	71
PS	93	32	53

T A B L E **3-6b**

No comment was made regarding the manager's relationship to the CEO. (227)

Type	Number	% of 227	% of Group
Mfg	32	14	34
Svc	98	43	50
NFP	15	7	29
PS	82	36	47

T A B L E **3-6c**

Don't jump to the conclusion that the manager does not want to hire women—have a meeting with him and discuss his interview notes. (242)

Type	Number	% of 242	% of Group
Mfg	57	24	61
Svc	49	20	25
NFP	7	3	13
PS	129	53	74

T A B L E **3-6d**

Proactively respond to the situation if there is a prima facie case for discrimination based on sex. (189)

Type	Number	% of 189	% of Group
Mfg	48	25	51
Svc	61	32	31
NFP	17	9	33
PS	63	33	36

T A B L E **3-6e**

Proactively respond to the situation because you do not want to be sued for helping the manager discriminate based on sex. (36)

Type	Number	% of 36	% of Group
Mfg	6	17	6
Svc	13	36	7
NFP	7	19	13
PS	10	28	6

T A B L E **3-6f**

Discuss the implications of the situation with manager, even if you do not believe discrimination is occurring; attempt to educate and counsel the manager about cultural differences between the United States and his native county. (130)

Type	Number	% of 130	% of Group
Mfg	29	22	31
Svc	67	52	34
NFP	16	12	31
PS	18	14	10

T A B L E **3-6g**

Outline together criteria for jobs that become available and encourage the manager to focus on these criteria. Review his interview notes prior to hiring and determine if the manager's recommendation is based on the criteria. (35)

Type	Number	% of 35	% of Group
Mfg	6	17	6
Svc	11	31	6
NFP	4	11	8
PS	14	40	8

T A B L E **3-6h**

Have the manager attend diversity training. (67)

Type	Number	% of 67	% of Group
Mfg	10	15	11
Svc	36	54	18
NFP	8	12	15
PS	13	19	7

T A B L E **3-6i**

Discuss the situation and potential damage to the company with senior management. Attempt to get their support about appropriate hiring practices from now on. (34)

Type	Number	% of 34	% of Group
Mfg	14	41	15
Svc	12	35	6
NFP	3	9	6
PS	5	15	3

T A B L E **3-6j**

Sit in on future interviews with the manager so you can determine if he needs coaching in interview practices. (44)

Type	Number	% of 44	% of Group
Mfg	12	27	13
Svc	29	66	15
NFP	3	7	6
PS	0	0	0

TABLE **3-6k**

If the manager does not change, go to the CEO and discuss the potential Title VII impact and why it is important to use objective hiring criteria. (92)

Type	Number	% of 92	% of Group
Mfg	38	41	40
Svc	40	43	20
NFP	8	9	15
PS	6	7	3

TABLE **3-6l**

If the CEO does not respond by supporting HR, the HR person should quit. (19)

Type	Number	% of 19	% of Group
Mfg	8	42	8.5
Svc	4	21	2
NFP	1	5	2
PS	6	32	3

The HR person should document steps taken and keep the documentation at home. (38)

Type	Number	% of 19	% of Group
Mfg	18	47	19
Svc	11	29	6
NFP	0	0	0
PS	9	24	5

Verbally go on record with the CEO that you disapprove of the manager's hiring practices. (23)

Type	Number	% of 19	% of Group
Mfg	4	17	4
Svc	8	35	4
NFP	3	13	6
PS	8	35	5

Continue trying to change the manager's hiring practices. (12)

Type	Number	% of 12	% of Group
Mfg	0	0	0
Svc	6	50	3
NFP	4	33	8
PS	2	17	1

TABLE **3-6m**

Review other units within the company to determine if adverse impact of any kind is taking place. If yes, conduct training on hiring and selection. (39)

Type	Number	% of 39	% of Group
Mfg	12	31	13
Svc	19	49	10
NFP	1	3	2
PS	7	4	4

TABLE **3-6n**

The HR person should take this situation as an indicator that HR must become educated about cultural differences in order to handle similar situations that arise. (14)

Type	Number	% of 14	% of Group
Mfg	2	14	2
Svc	3	21	1.5
NFP	2	14	4
PS	7	50	4

TABLE **3-7** Breakdown by Organization Size

Category	Number of Employees	Number
1	0–100	29
2	101–500	73
3	501–1,000	159
4	1,001–5,000	136
5	5,001–10,000	21

TABLE **3-7a**

Disregard the fact that the manager is related to the CEO. (291)

Category	Number	% of 291	% of Group
1	19	7	65.5
2	46	16	63
3	79	27	50
4	63	22	46
5	84	29	69

T A B L E **3-7b**

No comment was made regarding manager's relationship to the CEO. (227)

Category	Number	% of 227	% of Group
1	10	4	34.5
2	27	12	37
3	80	35	50
4	73	32	54
5	37	16	31

T A B L E **3-7c**

Don't jump to the conclusion that the manager does not want to hire women in these positions—have a meeting with him, discuss his interview notes, and investigate why he is rejecting women. (242)

Category	Number	% of 242	% of Group
1	13	5	45
2	49	20	67
3	98	40	62
4	59	24	43
5	23	10	19

T A B L E **3-7d**

Proactively respond to the situation if there is a prima facie case of discrimination based on sex. (189)

Category	Number	% of 189	% of Group
1	7	4	24
2	16	8	22
3	31	16	19
4	70	37	51
5	65	34	54

TABLE **3-7e**

Proactively respond to the situation because you do not want to be sued for helping the manager discriminate based on sex. (36)

Category	Number	% of 36	% of Group
1	7	19	24
2	9	25	12
3	12	33	7.5
4	0	0	0
5	8	22	22

TABLE **3-7f**

Discuss the implications of the situation with the manager, even if you do not believe there is discrimination occurring; attempt to counsel the manager about cultural differences between the United States and his native country. (130)

Category	Number	% of 130	% of Group
1	3	2	10
2	11	8	15
3	18	14	11
4	57	44	42
5	41	32	34

TABLE **3-7g**

Outline together criteria for jobs that become available and encourage the manager to focus on these criteria. Review his interview notes prior to hiring and determine if the manager's recommendation is based on the criteria. (35)

Category	Number	% of 35	% of Group
1	7	20	24
2	9	26	12
3	6	17	4
4	8	23	6
5	5	14	4

T A B L E **3-7h**

Have the manager attend diversity training. (67)

Category	Number	% of 67	% of Group
1	3	4	10
2	9	13	12
3	8	12	5
4	19	28	14
5	28	42	23

T A B L E **3-7i**

Sit in on future interviews with the manager so you can determine if he needs coaching on interview practices. (44)

Category	Number	% of 44	% of Group
1	7	16	24
2	9	20	12
3	6	14	4
4	10	23	7
5	12	27	10

T A B L E **3-7j**

Discuss the situation and potential damage to the company with senior management. Attempt to get their support about appropriate hiring practices from now on. (34)

Category	Number	% of 34	% of Group
1	7	21	24
2	16	47	22
3	3	9	2
4	0	0	0
5	8	24	7

T A B L E **3-7k**

If the manager does not change, go to the CEO and discuss the potential Title VII impact. (92)

Category	Number	% of 92	% of Group
1	17	18	59
2	39	42	53

T A B L E **3-7k** (continued)

Category	Number	% of 92	% of Group
3	19	21	12
4	15	16	11
5	2	2	2

T A B L E **3-7l**

If the CEO does not respond by supporting Human Resources, the HR person must quit. (19)

Category	Number	% of 19	% of Group
1	3	16	10
2	5	26	7
3	8	42	5
4	1	5	1
5	2	11	2

The HR person should document steps and keep a copy of documentation at home. (38)

Category	Number	% of 38	% of Group
1	2	5	7
2	4	11	5
3	12	32	7.5
4	12	32	9
5	8	21	7

Verbally go on record with the CEO that you disapprove of the manager's hiring practices. (23)

Category	Number	% of 23	% of Group
1	0	0	0
2	3	13	4
3	12	52	7.5
4	1	4	1
5	7	30	6

Continue trying to change the manager's hiring practices. (12)

Category	Number	% of 12	% of Group
1	1	8	3
2	3	25	4
3	0	0	0
4	2	17	1
5	6	50	5

TABLE **3-7m**

Review other units within the company to determine if adverse impact of any kind is taking place. If yes, conduct training on hiring and selection. (39)

Category	Number	% of 39	% of Group
1	0	0	0
2	4	10	5
3	19	49	12
4	11	28	8
5	5	13	4

TABLE **3-7n**

The HR person should take this situation as an indicator that HR must be educated about cultural differences. (14)

Category	Number	% of 14	% of Group
1	0	0	0
2	2	14	3
3	0	0	0
4	4	29	3
5	8	57	7

Nearly three-fourths of the not-for-profit respondents believe the manager's relationship to the CEO should not be a factor in the Human Resource professional's decision. Many in this group offer that they find it difficult to relate to the power held by a CEO in industry because such a position does not exist in the nonprofit sector. These respondents did, however, equate the position of CEO to a title such as Executive Director and answered the dilemma within that framework. A high percentage (66%) of manufacturing respondents also believe that the manager–CEO relationship should be disregarded, and this is a group that can more likely relate to the influence a CEO could have in an organization.

Just under three-fourths of the public sector respondents caution that Human Resources should not jump to the conclusion that the manager is purposely discriminating against women, compared with 25% of service organization respondents and 13% of nonprofit respondents. Typical public sector organizations represented in the survey are courts and probation offices, where the philosophical approach to work is one of investigation and due diligence. This demographic may account for the cautious attitude.

Respondents in the manufacturing group are more likely than representatives from the other types of organizations to take this issue directly to senior management or the CEO.

The distribution across manufacturing, service, and public sector respondents is fairly even with regard to the need to proactively respond *if* there appears to be evidence of discrimination based on sex. The group most concerned about personally being named in a lawsuit is the segment from service organizations. No research is currently available regarding lawsuits filed against Human Resource Managers from marketing as opposed to service organizations, although a trend has emerged for plaintiff's attorneys to name Human Resources Managers in Title VII, **Age Discrimination in Employment Act (ADEA), Family and Medical Leave Act (FMLA),** and ADA lawsuits. Research indicates that plaintiff's attorneys believe naming individuals will put additional pressure on companies to settle cases, according to Scott L. Fredericksen in a January 1997 white paper for the Society for Human Resource Management (www. shrm.org).

Eight of the 19 respondents who would resign if the CEO does not support Human Resources are from manufacturing companies. This sector also has the largest percentage that would document steps taken and keep these records at home. The degree of trust within a manufacturing environment and other industry sectors would make an interesting case study for future research.

3-5b Breakdown by Organization Size

If an organization has fewer than 500 employees, the likelihood that Human Resources is located at headquarters and is known by management staff is high. In larger organizations, however, HR staff may simply be names on an organization chart to most line managers. The level of influence individuals within Human Resources in large organizations perceive they possess with regard to managers may be minimal. Breezing into the CEO's office for a frequent chat is definitely not an option.

There are indeed some differences worth noting across respondents representing companies of varying sizes. Twenty-nine percent of the 291 respondents that believe Human Resources should disregard the manager's relationship with the CEO represent organizations that have between 5,001 and 10,000 employees. In an organization this large, it's likely that Human Resources staff do not have a personal relationship with the CEO. In fact, the HR staff may not ever meet the CEO in a company of this size. Because of this geographic and/or functional distance, it is less likely that individuals within HR would feel visible and exposed to the anger or displeasure of the CEO.

Respondents from organizations of less than 100 employees are most likely to respond to this situation proactively to avoid being named in a lawsuit. That is understandable—it is difficult to hide in such a small company!

Over half of the respondents from organizations of 1,001 to 5,000 employees and 5,001 to 10,000 employees suggest that HR should address this dilemma proactively if investigation reveals a prima facie case of discrimination based on sex. Larger companies may be perceived as having "deep pockets" when it comes to litigation, so this finding is not surprising.

Over 100 respondents suggest that a discussion should be held with the manager around cultural differences—differences that may affect his hiring decisions. Respondents from the two largest organization categories most frequently make this suggestion, making comments such as "an individual's cultural biases can adversely affect the entire company." Respondents from the larger companies are also those who make the suggestion most often to arrange for diversity training for the manager. Companies with 1,000-plus employees are typically in a better financial position to offer diversity training and may have a larger Human Resources staff that can provide one-on-one coaching on the topic of cultural diversity.

Almost one-fourth of respondents from companies with 100 or fewer employees recommend discussing the hiring situation with senior managers and soliciting their support for appropriate hiring practices. A higher percentage of respondents from this group also suggests discussing potential Title VII implications with the CEO, if necessary. A smaller company provides the advantage of more opportunities for Human Resources to connect with senior managers and the CEO, which may account for this finding.

If the CEO is not responsive to HR's concerns, respondents in companies with 501 to 1,000 employees are the most likely to recommend that the HR person should resign, document steps taken, or verbally go on record with regard to disapproving of the manager's hiring practices.

These findings suggest different approaches from individuals across organization size and industry sector. Nonprofit and manufacturing respondents are less influenced by the manager's relationship to a high-level executive than are other respondents. Public sector respondents are most likely to take a cautious approach toward handling this dilemma, and manufacturing respondents are most inclined toward documenting steps taken. Respondents from larger companies are more concerned about legal liability for the company, while smaller company representatives are more concerned about personal liability.

Chapter Summary

HR professionals are familiar with the legal issues in this scenario: potential discrimination; in this instance, based on sex. Unfortunately, we also have a predicament in that the "offender" is related to the keeper of our job, the CEO!

My biggest surprise in reviewing responses is that such a large percentage chose not to comment about the manager's relationship to the CEO. To me, this is like ignoring the elephant in the middle of the living room! I believe that tricky situations like this occur every day in the Human Resources profession, and we must take a position and be willing to "go public" with our views.

Even though only a few respondents take the approach of partnering with a manager who apparently needs one-on-one counseling, I have seen evidence in organizations across the United States that coaching is a growing trend. I view coaching as an excellent way for HR professionals to strongly impact an organization's culture.

Interesting differences are apparent across demographic groups, most notably between Caucasian and African American respondents. African American responses demonstrate a high degree of understanding around potential discrimination, perhaps because of personal experiences. We can all learn from this: There is probably at least one time in each of our lives when we felt left out or treated differently from the majority. It is not a good feeling, and I do not want to work for a company that condones intentional or unintentional discrimination.

More men than women in our response set urged caution against jumping immediately to the conclusion that the manager is purposely discriminating against women. As human beings, we draw conclusions based on personal experiences. As HR professionals, I believe our conclusions must be grounded on facts and perspectives offered by everyone involved in a given situation.

Discussion Questions

1. Would you quit your position if the CEO refused to take action against a person who is harming the company? Why or why not?
2. Are the rights of the hiring manager in this scenario to select staff for his department more or less important than the company's right to protect itself?
3. Is the Human Resource professional's first obligation to protect the interests of the company as a whole or the interests of the Human Resources Department? What are the interests of the Human Resources Department?

Chapter 4

Ethical Dilemma #2: A Supervisor Has HIV and Is a Gay-Rights Activist— Who Has a Right to Know?

Key Terms

AIDS	Generation Yers
Gay-rights activist	HIV

Outline

4-1 Breakdown by Total
4-2 Breakdown by Race and Ethnicity
4-3 Breakdown by Gender
4-4 Breakdown by Number of Years in Human Resources
4-5 Breakdown by Age
4-6 Breakdown by Organization Type
4-7 Breakdown by Organization Size
Chapter Summary
Discussion Questions

A first-line supervisor within an organization has tested positive for **HIV.** *He has advised Human Resources of this fact and that he intends to become a vocal community* **gay-rights activist.** *He indicated that he does not plan to disclose his diagnosis with coworkers. Who should Human Resources advise within the organization about this employee's illness and activist plans?*

In this scenario, Human Resources is faced with walking a fine line between protecting the privacy of an individual employee and protecting coworkers and the public. The specter of **AIDS** was not a concern for HR professionals 25 years ago, but the issue is one many Human Resource practitioners are faced with today. According to United Nations statistics (www.unaids.org), at the end of 2000 there were 920,000 adults and children living with HIV/AIDS in North America. An estimated 700,000 adults became infected with HIV or AIDS in South and Southeast Asia during 2000. The region of East Asia and the Pacific Rim had an estimated 640,000 people living with HIV or AIDS at the end of 2000.

I believe the discussion among Human Resource professionals must move beyond the employees' rights under the Americans With Disabilities Act and also consider these ethical questions:

- Which people within the company have a legitimate right to know about the supervisor's HIV status?
- Which people within the company have a legitimate right to know that the supervisor plans to take an activist role in gay rights?
- Does the fact that the employee is a first-line supervisor affect how Human Resources approaches this dilemma?

4-1 Breakdown by Total

Let's first take a look at the breakdown by all 518 respondents (Table 4-1), then explore how different demographic groups think about this issue.

TABLE **4-1**   Breakdown by Total

Two issues in scenario	9%
Disclose illness only to those at risk	58%
Do not disclose illness to anyone	31%
Disclose illness to all coworkers	10%
Do not disclose activism to anyone	36%
HR should monitor activism/take action if appropriate	37%

A small number of respondents sees two distinct issues within this scenario. This group perceives the HIV status of the supervisor as one issue and his activist plans as a separate concern. This response set approaches the scenario by making recommendations for addressing each issue.

A majority of respondents suggests that the supervisor's HIV status should be disclosed only to those who are at risk and therefore have a legitimate need to know about his illness. This group cites health care workers or coworkers who might come to his assistance in the event of injury as examples of people with a need for this knowledge. A concern raised by a small percentage (12%) of these 299 respondents is that the coworkers or third parties who (legitimately) obtain this information may purposely or inadvertently disclose it to others. They suggest that Human Resources should be firm in its communication about confidentiality to parties with whom this sensitive information is shared and should establish sanctions for inappropriate disclosures.

Almost one-third of the respondents recommend against disclosing the supervisor's HIV status to *any* coworkers, stating that he has a right to privacy. This group believes an individual's right to privacy in this circumstance overrides the company's (or coworkers') need to be aware of the illness. Some respondents in this group suggest, however, that the supervisor be transferred to another department or division if his presence places customers or coworkers at risk.

Ten percent of the respondents believe that the supervisor should disclose his illness to *all* coworkers because each coworker should have the right to take appropriate safeguards. Nine respondents in this group also recommend company-wide training to prevent mass hysteria.

Overall, respondents clearly take a view that the employee's activist plans do not pose a serious threat to the company. Just over one-third advises not to disclose the supervisor's anticipated activism to anyone within the company. This group also recommends that no action against the supervisor is warranted simply because he has indicated an interest in activism. In other words, the rights of the individual prevail over company interests in this particular case.

Sixteen percent of respondents recommend that only senior managers be advised of the supervisor's activist status, to provide them with a "heads up" about potential media coverage or negative publicity. This step, they believe, balances individual privacy rights against the company's need to take steps to foster a positive public image.

Just under 40% of the respondents suggest that Human Resources should be alert to whether the supervisor's activist role begins to impinge on work time or damage the company in any way. If either eventuality occurs, this group believes that Human Resources must request that the supervisor refrain from gay activism.

I am disappointed that only a small percentage of respondents feels that personal concern for the supervisor should be demonstrated by providing access to employee counseling. They believe this is the right thing to do and may help the supervisor to remain productive during a devastating personal experience.

4-2 Breakdown by Race and Ethnicity

One might expect different reactions to this dilemma across age, ethnic, and gender groups, and this certainly is the case. Table 4-2 explores the differences across racial and ethnic groups.

TABLE **4-2a**

There are two issues within this scenario: one, the HIV status of the supervisor and two, the activist plans. (48)

Category	Number	% of 48	% of Group
Caucasian	33	69	10
African American	8	17	6
Asian	2	4	5
Hispanic	5	10	19

TABLE **4-2b**

Disclose the employee's HIV status only to those at risk and who have a need to know about the illness. (299)

Category	Number	% of 299	% of Group
Caucasian	170	57	54
African American	88	29	65
Asian	26	9	63
Hispanic	15	5	58

TABLE **4-2c**

Make a reasonable accommodation for the employee, if required, such as transfer to a different department/division. (16)

Category	Number	% of 16	% of Group
Caucasian	9	56	3
African American	0	0	0
Asian	2	13	5
Hispanic	5	31	19

TABLE **4-2d**

Do not disclose his HIV status to coworkers; the employee has a right to privacy. (160)

Category	Number	% of 160	% of Group
Caucasian	101	63	32
African American	39	24	29
Asian	12	8	29
Hispanic	8	5	31

TABLE **4-2e**

Advise the employee's immediate supervisor of his HIV status so this person can take appropriate steps. (16)

Category	Number	% of 16	% of Group
Caucasian	7	44	2
African American	4	25	3
Asian	3	19	7
Hispanic	2	13	8

TABLE **4-2f**

Advise the employee to disclose his HIV status and counsel on how to do this. (77)

Category	Number	% of 77	% of Group
Caucasian	52	68	16
African American	14	18	10
Asian	2	3	5
Hispanic	9	12	35

T A B L E **4-2g**

Disclose to all employees the fact that the employee has HIV; they have a right to know and take precautions. (52)

Category	Number	% of 52	% of Group
Caucasian	19	36.5	6
African American	26	50	19
Asian	6	11.5	15
Hispanic	1	2	4

T A B L E **4-2h**

The employee's activist activities are his business; do not disclose to anyone or take any action against the employee. (186)

Category	Number	% of 186	% of Group
Caucasian	70	38	22
African American	73	39	54
Asian	28	15	68
Hispanic	15	8	58

T A B L E **4-2i**

If the employee's activist role begins to impinge on work time or damage the company in some way, HR should ask the employee to refrain from these activities. (191)

Category	Number	% of 191	% of Group
Caucasian	78	41	25
African American	60	31	44
Asian	31	16	76
Hispanic	22	12	85

T A B L E **4-2j**

Advise senior managers within the company of the employee's activist activities to give them a "heads up." (81)

Category	Number	% of 81	% of Group
Caucasian	39	48	12
African American	32	40	24
Asian	6	7	15
Hispanic	4	5	15

TABLE **4-2k**

Show concern for the employee. Encourage him to use the Employee Assistance Program (EAP) or outside counseling services. (15)

Category	Number	% of 15	% of Group
Caucasian	7	47	2
African American	5	33	4
Asian	0	0	0
Hispanic	3	20	11.5

The majority of the 48 respondents who believe there are two distinct issues in this scenario (the supervisor's HIV status and the anticipated activism) is Caucasian (69%). However, more Hispanics as a percentage of demographic group (19%) treat this dilemma as two separate concerns than any other demographic group.

Most respondents want to keep disclosure to a minimum number of people. Caucasians comprise the largest group overall and the largest percentage of the demographic group that does *not* want to disclose the supervisor's HIV status to coworkers. Many of the comments from this group revolve around the supervisor's right to privacy in the face of this serious illness and not feeding the fear that still exists about the risk of contagion.

Sixty-five percent of the total African American response group and 63% of the total Asian response group want to disclose only to those at risk, compared to 58% of Hispanics and 54% of Caucasians.

The number of respondents within the population that suggests advising the supervisor's manager of his illness is small, and Asians and Hispanics represent the largest percentage of their demographic groups who suggest letting the supervisor's immediate manager handle the situation. These respondents suggest that HR should not overstep its boundaries and intercede in the place of an employee's immediate supervisor. The response from Asian practitioners takes me back to ethical dilemma #1, wherein many of our Asian respondents note an awareness of Human Resource positions in many companies as being at a lower level than most line managers.

Just over one-third of the Hispanic respondents indicate the best course of action is to advise the supervisor to disclose his illness. This group suggests that getting the facts out directly and in a straightforward manner is the appropriate way to proceed. An Hispanic colleague who provided me with insights into his culture advised me that, in his culture, being straightforward and open is a valued trait.

African Americans represent half of the respondents overall and the largest percentage of demographic group (19%) that believes Human Resources should disclose the supervisor's illness to all employees. For this group, the needs of the many within the organizational community take precedence over an individual's right to privacy.

In light of the Japanese culture's view of organizations, a surprisingly high percentage (68%) of Asian respondents asserts that the supervisor's activism is his own concern, not that of the company. This group does not believe activist involvement should be disclosed to anyone, nor should Human Resources intervene with the supervisor to attempt to convince him to curtail these activities. Of the 28 respondents who offer this opinion, 89% represent companies with more than 1,000 employees. This may account for their perception that one person's activities will not significantly impact the organization. Seventy-six percent of the Asian respondents want to intervene *only* if the activities begin to damage the company. The Asian respect for the good of the company as a whole is evidenced in this response.

Eighty-five percent of the Hispanic respondents believe that Human Resources should intervene with the supervisor's activism only if his activities begin to damage the company in some way. The theme emerging from this response group's answers is one of treating the supervisor with respect so that whenever he is in a public arena, he will speak positively about the organization.

4-3 Breakdown by Gender

Because of socialization and different experiences in the workplace, I expected that responses would be different between men and women, and our respondents did not disappoint me (Table 4-3)!

T A B L E **4-3a**

There are two issues within this scenario: one, the HIV status and two, the activist plans. (48)

Group	Number	% of 48	% of Group
Male	17	35	10
Female	31	65	9

TABLE **4-3b**

Disclose the employee's HIV status only to those at risk and who have a need to know about the illness (health care/food handlers/person helping him if injured). (299)

Group	Number	% of 299	% of Group
Male	106	35	64
Female	193	65	55

TABLE **4-3c**

Make a reasonable accommodation for the employee, if required, such as a transfer to a different department/division. (16)

Group	Number	% of 16	% of Group
Male	4	25	2
Female	12	75	3

TABLE **4-3d**

Do not disclose his HIV status to coworkers; the employee has a right to privacy. (160)

Group	Number	% of 160	% of Group
Male	71	44	43
Female	89	56	25

TABLE **4-3e**

Advise the employee's immediate supervisor of his HIV status so that this person can take appropriate steps. (16)

Group	Number	% of 16	% of Group
Male	6	37.5	4
Female	10	62.5	3

TABLE **4-3f**

Advise the employee to disclose his HIV status and counsel on how to do this. (77)

Group	Number	% of 77	% of Group
Male	25	32	15
Female	34	68	15

T A B L E **4-3g**

Disclose to all coworkers the fact that the employee has HIV; they have a right to know and take precautions. (52)

Group	Number	% of 52	% of Group
Male	18	35	11
Female	34	65	10

T A B L E **4-3h**

The employee's activist activities are his business; do not disclose to anyone or take any action against the employee. (186)

Group	Number	% of 186	% of Group
Male	84	45	51
Female	102	55	29

T A B L E **4-3i**

If the employee's activist role begins to impinge on work time or damage the company, HR should ask the employee to refrain from these activities. (191)

Group	Number	% of 191	% of Group
Male	79	41	48
Female	102	59	42

T A B L E **4-3j**

Advise senior managers within the company of the employee's activist status to give them a "heads up." (81)

Group	Number	% of 81	% of Group
Male	22	27	13
Female	59	73	17

T A B L E **4-3k**

Show concern for the employee. Encourage him to use the EAP or outside counseling services. (15)

Group	Number	% of 15	% of Group
Male	2	13	1
Female	13	87	4

My expectation prior to conducting the survey was that men would be especially sensitive to individual privacy rights because, at this point, more men in the United States than women suffer from HIV or AIDS, according to available Centers for Disease Control statistics (www.bu. edu). I believe the concern from women in this country will escalate, however, because women are one of the fastest-growing groups of new AIDS cases, accounting for 20% of newly reported cases in the United States in 1996 (www.fwhc.org).

Sixty-four percent of male respondents suggest that only those at risk should be advised of the supervisor's illness. Fewer (55%) female respondents believe this is the appropriate way to handle the situation. Forty-three percent of the male respondents recommend against disclosing the supervisor's HIV status to coworkers, compared to one-fourth of female respondents. Common male comments in this group are, "Disclosure might trigger anti-gay, negative reactions," and "This person's illness is his business." Our female respondents had very similar arguments against disclosure.

The percentages of recommendations about informing the employee's immediate manager, advising the employee to disclose his illness, and disclosing the illness to all coworkers are similar for men and women. Some significant differences can be noted between the sexes, however, with regard to gay rights activities.

Fifty-one percent of the male respondents assert that the supervisor's activism is his personal choice and that Human Resources should take no action on this point. Only 29% of the female respondents provide this response. However, 48% of the men suggest action should be taken if the activism damages the company, as opposed to 32% of the women. The men in our sample are more reluctant than the women to intervene unless and until the supervisor's activism adversely affects the company.

4-4 Breakdown by Number of Years in Human Resources

Table 4-4 looks at differences in responses by the number of years in Human Resources.

T A B L E **4-4a**

There are two issues within this scenario: one, the HIV status of the supervisor and two, the activist plans. (48)

Tenure	Number	% of 48	% of Group
0–1	2	4	2
2–3	6	12.5	6
4–5	10	21	17
6–10	12	25	7
> 10	18	37.5	19

T A B L E **4-4b**

Disclose the employee's HIV status only to those at risk and who have a need to know about the illness. (299)

Tenure	Number	% of 299	% of Group
0–1	45	15	51
2–3	46	15	45
4–5	33	11	57
6–10	128	43	73
> 10	47	16	51

T A B L E **4-4c**

Make a reasonable accommodation for the employee, if required, such as a transfer to a different department/division. (16)

Tenure	Number	% of 16	% of Group
0–1	1	6	1
2–3	3	19	3
4–5	0	0	0
6–10	4	25	2
> 10	8	50	9

T A B L E **4-4d**

Do not disclose his HIV status to coworkers; the employee has a right to privacy. (160)

Tenure	Number	% of 160	% of Group
0–1	44	28	49
2–3	50	31	49

T A B L E **4-4d** *(continued)*

Tenure	Number	% of 160	% of Group
4–5	23	14	40
6–10	34	21	19
> 10	9	6	10

T A B L E **4-4e**

Advise the employee's immediate supervisor of his HIV status so that this person can take appropriate steps. (16)

Tenure	Number	% of 16	% of Group
0–1	5	31	6
2–3	4	25	4
4–5	2	12.5	3
6–10	3	19	1
> 10	2	12.5	2

T A B L E **4-4f**

Advise the employee to disclose his HIV status and counsel on how to do this. (77)

Tenure	Number	% of 77	% of Group
0–1	6	8	7
2–3	8	10	8
4–5	12	16	21
6–10	14	18	8
> 10	37	48	40

T A B L E **4-4g**

Disclose to all coworkers the fact that the employee has HIV; they have a right to know and take precautions. (52)

Tenure	Number	% of 52	% of Group
0–1	0	0	0
2–3	6	12	6
4–5	2	4	3
6–10	14	27	8
> 10	30	58	32

T A B L E **4-4h**

The employee's activist activities are his business; do not disclose to anyone or take any action against the employee. (186)

Tenure	Number	% of 186	% of Group
0–1	43	23	48
2–3	57	31	56
4–5	31	17	53
6–10	29	16	16
> 10	26	14	28

T A B L E **4-4i**

If the employee's activist role begins to impinge on work time or damage the company in some way, HR should ask the employee to refrain from these activities. (191)

Tenure	Number	% of 191	% of Group
0–1	43	23	48
2–3	38	20	37
4–5	26	14	45
6–10	49	26	28
> 10	35	18	38

T A B L E **4-4j**

Advise senior managers within the company of the employee's activist status to give them a "heads up." (81)

Tenure	Number	% of 81	% of Group
0–1	30	37	34
2–3	37	46	36
4–5	11	14	19
6–10	3	4	2
> 10	0	0	0

T A B L E **4-4k**

Show concern for the employee. Encourage him to use the EAP or outside counseling services. (15)

Tenure	Number	% of 15	% of Group
0–1	6	40	7
2–3	4	27	4

T A B L E **4-4k** *(continued)*

Tenure	Number	% of 15	% of Group
4–5	3	20	5
6–10	0	0	0
> 10	2	13	2

4-5 Breakdown by Age

Table 4-5 looks at differences in responses based on age.

T A B L E **4-5a**

There are two issues within this scenario: one, the HIV status of the supervisor and two, the activist plans. (48)

Age	Number	% of 48	% of Group
< 30	8	17	4
31–40	22	46	9
41–50	11	23	18
51–60	7	15	21

T A B L E **4-5b**

Disclose the employee's HIV status only to those at risk and who have a need to know about the illness. (299)

Age	Number	% of 299	% of Group
< 30	91	30	48
31–40	161	54	69
41–50	17	6	28
51–60	30	10	91

T A B L E **4-5c**

Make a reasonable accommodation for the employee, if required, such as transfer to a different department/division. (16)

Age	Number	% of 16	% of Group
< 30	4	25	2
31–40	4	25	2
41–50	4	25	7
51–60	4	25	12

T A B L E **4-5d**

Do not disclose his HIV status to coworkers; the employee has a right to privacy. (160)

Age	Number	% of 160	% of Group
< 30	94	59	49
31–40	57	36	24
41–50	3	2	5
51–60	6	4	18

T A B L E **4-5e**

Advise the employee's immediate supervisor of his HIV status so that this person can take appropriate steps. (16)

Age	Number	% of 16	% of Group
< 30	9	56	5
31–40	5	31	2
41–50	2	13	3
51–60	0	0	0

T A B L E **4-5f**

Advise the employee to disclose his HIV status and counsel on how to do this. (77)

Age	Number	% of 77	% of Group
< 30	14	18	7
31–40	26	34	11
41–50	16	21	27
51–60	21	27	64

T A B L E **4-5g**

Disclose to all employees the fact that the employee has HIV; they have a right to know and take precautions. (52)

Age	Number	% of 52	% of Group
< 30	6	12	3
31–40	16	31	7
41–50	19	37	32
51–60	11	21	33

T A B L E **4-5h**

The employee's activist activities are his business; do not disclose to anyone or take any action against the employee. (186)

Age	Number	% of 186	% of Group
< 30	100	54	52
31–40	60	32	26
41–50	20	11	33
51–60	6	3	18

T A B L E **4-5i**

If the employee's activist role begins to impinge on work time or damage the company in some way, HR should ask the employee to refrain from these activities. (191)

Age	Number	% of 191	% of Group
< 30	81	42	42
31–40	75	39	32
41–50	16	8	27
51–60	19	10	58

T A B L E **4-5j**

Advise senior managers within the company of the employee's activist activities to give them a "heads up." (81)

Age	Number	% of 81	% of Group
< 30	67	83	35
31–40	14	17	6
41–50	0	0	0
51–60	0	0	0

T A B L E **4-5k**

Show concern for the employee. Encourage him to use the EAP or outside counseling services. (15)

Age	Number	% of 15	% of Group
< 30	10	67	5
31–40	3	20	1
41–50	2	13	3
51–60	0	0	0

I anticipated that the youngest (under age 30) HR practitioners would be supportive of activism because so many Generation Xers and **Generation Yers** (people born between 1977 and 1985) are themselves involved in grassroots efforts on behalf of social issues such as AIDS research (see www.emagazine.com/september-october 1999 and "The Echo-Boom," by Mark L. Alch,[1] *The Futurist,* September–October 2000).

The more tenured, older respondents are those who most often view this dilemma as having two components. Experience leads these people toward breaking down issues and looking at context rather than making a sweeping judgment about the best way to proceed.

The majority of respondents with 6 to 10 years of experience in Human Resources recommend that only coworkers and customers who are at risk should receive information about the supervisor's HIV status, compared to 51% of respondents with 1 year or less and over 10 years of experience. These respondents are making an effort to balance the rights of the individual (for privacy) with the rights of the many (for safety).

Nearly one-half of the respondents with under 3 years of HR experience argue that nobody should have access to information about the supervisor's illness. The majority of this response group is under age 30, a generation that, unfortunately, has grown up in a time when HIV and AIDS have taken the form of friends and neighbors as opposed to being cold statistics. Many of the comments from this group reflect the concern that homophobia is still alive in the United States and there is no need to unnecessarily generate hostility.

One-third of the respondents between ages 51 and 60 and 32% of respondents between 41 and 50 recommend disclosing the supervisor's HIV status to all coworkers. Sixty-four percent of respondents between 51 and 60 suggest that Human Resources should advise the supervisor to disclose his illness and should provide counseling about the best communication method. Comments across these two age groups focus on protecting the company's image and maintaining a safe environment.

With regard to gay rights activities, over half (52%) of respondents under age 30 insist that the supervisor has a right to become an activist without intervention, as opposed to only 18% of those between 51 and 60. Interestingly, 48% of respondents with 1 year or less experience (mostly under age 30) suggest that Human Resources must intervene if the supervisor's activism impinges on work time or damages the company, compared to 38% of those with more than 10 years' experience. Younger respondents are willing to stay out of the picture unless activism damages the company.

---

1. Alch, Mark L. 2000, September–October. "The Echo-Boom." *The Futurist,* pages 45–46.

4-6 Breakdown by Organization Type

Table 4-6 looks at differences in responses based on organization type.

TABLE **4-6a**

There are two issues with this scenario: one, the HIV status of the supervisor and two, the activist plans. (48)

Type	Number	% of 48	% of Group
Mfg	9	19	10
Svc	20	42	10
NFP	7	15	13
PS	12	25	7

TABLE **4-6b**

Disclose the employee's HIV status only to those at risk and who have a need to know about the illness. (299)

Type	Number	% of 299	% of Group
Mfg	69	23	73
Svc	83	28	42
NFP	31	10	60
PS	116	39	66

TABLE **4-6c**

Make a reasonable accommodation for the employee, if required, such as a transfer to another department/division. (16)

Type	Number	% of 16	% of Group
Mfg	4	25	4
Svc	5	31	2.5
NFP	0	0	0
PS	7	44	4

TABLE **4-6d**

Do not disclose his HIV status to coworkers; the employee has a right to privacy. (160)

Type	Number	% of 160	% of Group
Mfg	25	16	27
Svc	90	56	46
NFP	18	11	35
PS	27	17	15

TABLE **4-6e**

Advise the employee's immediate supervisor of his HIV status so that this person can take appropriate steps. (16)

Type	Number	% of 16	% of Group
Mfg	9	56	10
Svc	4	25	2
NFP	0	0	0
PS	3	19	2

TABLE **4-6f**

Advise the employee to disclose his HIV status and counsel on how to do this. (77)

Type	Number	% of 77	% of Group
Mfg	35	45	37
Svc	26	34	13
NFP	7	9	13
PS	9	12	5

TABLE **4-6g**

Disclose to all coworkers the fact that the employee has HIV; they have a right to know and take appropriate precautions. (52)

Type	Number	% of 52	% of Group
Mfg	6	12	6
Svc	11	21	6
NFP	20	38	38
PS	15	29	9

TABLE **4-6h**

The employee's activist activities are his business; do not disclose to anyone or take any action against the employee. (186)

Type	Number	% of 186	% of Group
Mfg	47	25	50
Svc	51	27	26
NFP	23	12	44
PS	65	35	37

TABLE **4-6i**

If the employee's activist role begins to impinge on work time or damage the company in some way, HR should ask the employee to refrain from these activities. (191)

Type	Number	% of 191	% of Group
Mfg	24	13	26
Svc	74	39	38
NFP	21	11	40
PS	72	38	41

TABLE **4-6j**

Advise senior managers within the company of the employee's activist status to give them a "heads up" about potential media coverage or exposure. (81)

Type	Number	% of 81	% of Group
Mfg	31	38	33
Svc	14	17	7
NFP	7	9	13
PS	29	36	17

TABLE **4-6k**

Show concern for the employee. Encourage him to use the EAP or outside counseling services. (15)

Type	Number	% of 15	% of Group
Mfg	2	13	2
Svc	5	33	2.5
NFP	5	33	10
PS	3	20	2

Because 42% of the not-for-profit organizations are within the health care field and 30% are in social work or counseling areas, I expected that these sectors would perceive an urgent need to protect coworkers and patients while showing empathy and support for the supervisor. They did not!

The number of respondents who suggest disclosing the illness to all coworkers is indeed small (52). The largest percentage (38%) comes from the not-for-profit respondents. Examples of comments from this group are: "Don't enable the supervisor to put others in danger" and "Protect innocent people from exposure." The supervisor's need for privacy is subordinate to coworker and client/patient safety.

The majority of manufacturing and public sector respondents believe the supervisor's HIV status should be disclosed *only* to those at risk. In a manufacturing environment or an office, these respondents indicated that there are fewer opportunities for exposure than there are in organizations such as health care or food preparation.

Forty-six percent of service company respondents believe that the supervisor's illness should not be disclosed to coworkers. This finding can be partially accounted for by the fact that one-third of the response group from service companies is under age 30, and I noted earlier that many in this age group believe in the supervisor's right to privacy.

Just over one-third of the manufacturing respondents suggest that Human Resources advise the supervisor to disclose his illness. These respondents feel that the supervisor is in the best position to identify those who have a legitimate "need to know."

Half of the manufacturing respondents and 44% of the not-for-profit respondents believe the supervisor's activism is his own business. These practitioners believe that one person's activities in this arena can do little to damage the organization, especially if it is a large company. Because not-for-profits rely heavily on private funding and grants, the 44% response rate in this category may surprise many readers. If an employee's activities reflect badly (or are perceived to reflect badly) on the organization, funding could be adversely affected. One-third of the manufacturing respondents, however, believe it is necessary to advise senior managers about the supervisor's activist role. The notice would simply be a "heads up" in the event his activities receive media coverage.

Forty-one percent of the public sector respondents suggest intervention by Human Resources if the supervisor's activism begins to impinge on work time or damages the organization. One perception that exists in the United States about public sector workers is that they do not care about using time productively. (I know this because I spent 9 years with public sector organizations.) Here is a group of public sector managers who do care about productivity.

4-7 Breakdown by Organization Size

Table 4-7 looks at the differences in responses based on organization size.

TABLE **4-7a**

There are two issues within this scenario: one, the HIV status of the supervisor and two, the activist plans. (48)

Category	Number	% of 48	% of Group
1	12	25	41
2	9	19	12
3	14	29	9
4	11	23	8
5	2	4	2

TABLE **4-7b**

Disclose the employee's HIV status only to those at risk and who have a need to know about the illness. (299)

Category	Number	% of 299	% of Group
1	18	6	62
2	59	20	81
3	97	32	61
4	83	28	61
5	42	14	35

TABLE **4-7c**

Make a reasonable accommodation for the employee, if required, such as a transfer to a different department/division. (16)

Category	Number	% of 16	% of Group
1	0	0	0
2	4	25	5
3	2	13	1
4	3	19	2
5	7	44	6

TABLE **4-7d**

Do not disclose his HIV status to coworkers; the employee has a right to privacy. (160)

Category	Number	% of 160	% of Group
1	10	6	34
2	12	8	16
3	61	38	38
4	60	38	44
5	17	11	14

TABLE **4-7e**

Advise the employee's immediate supervisor of his HIV status so that this person can take appropriate steps. (16)

Category	Number	% of 16	% of Group
1	1	6	3
2	4	25	5
3	4	25	2.5
4	0	0	0
5	7	44	6

TABLE **4-7f**

Advise the employee to disclose his HIV status and counsel on how to do this. (77)

Category	Number	% of 77	% of Group
1	2	3	7
2	24	31	33
3	10	13	6
4	13	17	10
5	28	36	23

TABLE **4-7g**

Disclose to all coworkers the fact that the employee has HIV; they have a right to know and to take appropriate precautions. (52)

Category	Number	% of 52	% of Group
1	3	6	10
2	8	15	11
3	24	46	15
4	10	19	7
5	7	13	6

TABLE **4-7h**

The employee's activist activities are his business; do not disclose to anyone or take any action against the employee. (186)

Category	Number	% of 186	% of Group
1	13	7	45
2	19	10	26
3	38	20	24
4	49	26	36
5	67	36	55

TABLE **4-7i**

If the employee's activist role begins to impinge on work time or damage the company in some way, HR should ask the employee to refrain from these activities. (191)

Category	Number	% of 191	% of Group
1	19	10	65.5
2	60	31	82
3	32	17	20
4	39	20	29
5	41	21	34

TABLE **4-7j**

Advise senior managers within the company of employee's activist status to give them a "heads up." (81)

Category	Number	% of 81	% of Group
1	12	15	41
2	42	52	57.5
3	16	20	10
4	8	10	6
5	3	4	2

TABLE **4-7k**

Show concern for the employee. Encourage him to use the EAP or outside counseling services. (15)

Category	Number	% of 15	% of Group
1	1	7	3
2	0	0	0
3	4	27	2.5
4	4	27	3
5	6	40	5

In a larger organization, anonymity is not assured; however, an employee is certainly less noticeable in a company of 9,000 employees than one with 98 employees. Therefore, I expected that practitioners from smaller companies would be less inclined to disclose the supervisor's illness.

Eighty-one percent of respondents from companies with 101 to 500 employees want to disclose the supervisor's illness only to those at risk. Many in this group worry about keeping rumors from flying in a small company and suggest sanctions against anyone who divulges this confidential information. One-third of respondents from companies with 101 to 500 employees recommend that the supervisor be advised to disclose his illness to those he deems appropriate.

Forty-four percent of respondents from companies with 1,001 to 5,000 employees believe the supervisor has a right to privacy and that no coworkers should be advised of his illness, compared to about one-third of respondents from companies with 501 to 1,000 employees. Many in the smaller companies suggest that keeping this type of news from coworkers is virtually impossible.

Fourteen percent of respondents representing the largest companies (5,001 to 10,000 employees) advise against disclosure to anyone. These respondents primarily cite potential damage to the company's public image as their reasoning for not disclosing the illness. This response begs the question, "What would the public think if a customer or coworker was (avoidably) exposed to risk because the illness was not disclosed?"

Over half of the respondents in 5,001 to 10,000 employee companies believe the supervisor's activism is his private choice, compared to 45% of companies with 100 or fewer employees. In very small or very large companies, then, a large number of our survey respondents feel that one's personal activities are not the company's affair. The smaller company representatives, however, believe that HR must intervene if the activities impinge on work time or damage the company. A smaller company is likely to be less able to absorb the impact of an unproductive employee, so this is not an unexpected finding.

Smaller company respondents are most likely to suggest that senior management be advised of the supervisor's activist status. These respondents cite negative publicity in the event of media coverage as a potential contributor to a loss of sales and jobs being jeopardized, and they believe managers must be prepared to handle this contingency.

Chapter Summary

In this scenario, Human Resource practitioners are forced to decide whether it is more important for them to protect employee privacy or sacrifice privacy for public safety. Human Resource professionals in this case must make a judgment call when they discover that employees have HIV or AIDS: which people have a legitimate right to know?

A majority of our respondents believe that the list of people who should be made aware of the supervisor's HIV status is a short one. Just under one-third of the response set does not even believe *anyone* should be provided with this knowledge. The HR professionals in this survey clearly weigh in on the side of employee privacy, at least when it comes to disclosing information about a serious illness. I would like to see surveys conducted posing a similar scenario except for a less deadly disease, to see if the opinions about privacy change. (Maybe I'll even conduct the surveys!) My personal belief is that *any* employee illness or medical condition is private and should only be disclosed to those who need to know. I understand that talking over such "juicy" pieces of information at the water cooler is tempting; however, leadership in the organization must clearly set the example in this type of situation.

Most of our respondents do not view the supervisor's activist plans as a major threat to the company. Over one-third does not think his activist plans should even be discussed with anyone within the company, although respondents do usually suggest that Human Resources monitor the situation in the event the supervisor's activism becomes a problem. If this situation occurs within *your* organization, I think an in-depth discussion within the leadership ranks must take place to ascertain exactly what "becoming a problem" means.

Differences in responses across demographic groups are evident with this scenario. Caucasians comprise the largest group overall and the largest percentage of their demographic group that does not think the supervisor's HIV status should be disclosed to coworkers. A higher percentage of men than women believes disclosure should be limited to people at risk of exposure, and more men than women assert that the supervisor's activist plans are his private business. I have to wonder—if the supervisor in this scenario was a woman, would more women believe the illness should not be disclosed?

Nearly half of our respondents with less than 3 years of Human Resources experience (primarily people under age 30) assert that no one should have access to information about the supervisor's illness. This younger age group is also more likely to find that gay activism is the supervisor's personal decision and not an appropriate topic for discussion with others.

The organization type with the largest percentage that would disclose the illness to coworkers is not-for-profit. Manufacturing respondents comprise the highest group percentage that suggests the supervisor's HIV status should be shared only with those at risk of exposure. With regard to differences across organization size, respondents from smaller companies are most in favor of disclosing the supervisor's HIV status only to those at risk. Of course, the challenge for HR professionals in a small organization is keeping confidential matters just that—confidential.

Discussion Questions
Discussion Questions

1. Is an employee's illness a private matter that should not be shared with coworkers? Under what circumstances is breaching an individual's privacy warranted?

2. Is an organization's size or sector important in the decision-making process regarding disclosure about individuals' illnesses?

3. Should an employee's off-the-job activities be investigated and limited by an employer? Under what circumstances can an employee's outside activities be sanctioned?

Chapter 5

Ethical Dilemma #3: To Explore or Not to Explore a Rumor— That Is the Question

Key Terms

Acquisition
Good faith bargaining
Merger
National Labor Relations
Act (NLRA)

National Labor Relations
Board (NLRB)
Negotiations

Securities and Exchange
Commission (SEC)

Outline

5-1 Breakdown by Total
5-2 Breakdown by Race and Ethnicity
5-3 Breakdown by Gender
5-4 Breakdown by the Number of Years in Human Resources and Age
5-5 Breakdown by Organization Type
5-6 Breakdown by Organization Size
Chapter Summary
Discussion Questions

It is time for your organization to negotiate with the union for a new collective bargaining agreement. The union negotiator has requested information about potential mergers or sales of company divisions in preparation for **negotiations.** *You have heard a rumor that a large company is interested in a* **merger** *or even an* **acquisition** *of your company.*

Three significant issues arise in this scenario. First, what is HR's role in sourcing and verifying rumors? Second, how does Human Resources meet (and perhaps exceed) the legal concept of **"good faith bargaining"**? Third, is HR's obligation to protect the company's management prerogative or to serve as an employee advocate? As with our previous dilemmas, laws are on the books that cover some aspects of this situation. The specific law relevant in this case is the **National Labor Relations Act (NLRA)**, passed in 1935 and enforced by the **National Labor Relations Board (NLRB)**.

The pertinent NLRA section states that:

> "Upon the request of the union, the employer is required to furnish to the union any information relevant to the union's role as the exclusive representative of the employees, including certain information about non-bargaining unit employees. Requested information must be furnished if it is relevant either to the negotiation or administration of a collective bargaining agreement. . . ."[1]

---

1. *Detroit Edison Co. v. NLRB*, 440 U.S. 301, 100 LRRM 2728, 85 CCH LC Para 11129 (1979); Westinghouse Electric Corp., 239 NLRB 106, 99 LRRM 1482, 78–79 CCH LC Para 15191 (1978); Cincinnati Steel Castings Co., 86 NLRB 592, 24 LRRM 1657, 49–50 CCH LC Para 9323 (1949); Brazos Electric Power Cooperative, Inc. 241 NLRB 1016, 101 LRRM 1003, 78–79 CCH Para 15786 (1979), enf'd 615 F.2nd 1100, 104 LRRM 2123, 88 CCH LC Para 12024 (5th Cir. 1980); Westinghouse Electric Corp., N 148 supra.

The pivotal question is: If Human Resources complies with the letter of the law, is it also acting ethically? According to Lewicki and Litterer in *Negotiation*,[2]

> "…The information exchanged, and the 'common definition' of the situation that emerges, serves as a rationale for each side to modify its position, and to eventually accept a settlement." The information Human Resources researches and provides could have a serious impact on the outcome of the negotiations.

The authors of *Human Resource Management*[3] assert that "Another role unions fill is as a countervailing force that keeps management 'honest' and makes management consider the impact of its policies on its employees."

This mindset, in my opinion, sets the tone for an adversarial relationship between unions and management rather than a relationship built on trust.

5-1 Breakdown by Total

Table 5-1 shows the responses of our entire population of 518 to this scenario.

TABLE **5-1** Breakdown by Total

HR should disregard rumor	59%
HR should explore the rumor	34%
Uncertain about HR's role	7%
Explore to keep HR advised of key events	4%

Fifty-nine percent of respondents believe the rumor should be totally disregarded! They feel that, if no facts are presented through appropriate channels, HR need not take time to source and investigate rumors. This group suggests that staff's time can be more productively spent in activities such as recruiting, training, and payroll.

Just over one-third (34%) of respondents believe that HR should explore the rumor and determine if it is true or false. This group recommends sharing the information with the union *if* it can be verified as

2. Lewicki, Roy J., and Litterer, Joseph A. 1985. *Negotiation*. Homewood, IL: Irwin Publishing, pages 14, 324.

3. *Human Resources Management*, 7th edition. West Publishing, page 207.

accurate. These respondents feel that taking time to verify the rumor follows the spirit of "good faith bargaining," in part because there is a strong likelihood that union representatives have also heard the rumor.

I am disappointed to report that only 23 respondents (4%) recommend that HR explore the rumor because the department needs to be aware of potential mergers or acquisitions for its own strategic planning purposes. This group believes that Human Resources must position itself as a strategic planning partner to guide the organization in making appropriate staffing and employee development decisions. Once Human Resources verifies the accuracy of the rumor, these respondents believe, a decision can be made about what disclosure tactics should be employed, and when.

5-2 Breakdown by Race and Ethnicity

Table 5-2 series shows the breakdown of responses by race and ethnicity. I found some distinct differences in responses across the four racial and ethnic categories of respondents.

TABLE **5-2a**

Disregard the rumor being spread—it is only a rumor. (307)

Category	Number	% of 307	% of Group
Caucasian	232	75	73
African American	69	22	51
Asian	5	2	12
Hispanic	1	<1	4

TABLE **5-2b**

Explore the rumor and advise the union rep what you discover (if true), because the union has probably heard it too—this is good faith bargaining. (177)

Category	Number	% of 177	% of Group
Caucasian	69	39	22
African American	58	33	43
Asian	30	17	73
Hispanic	20	11	77

TABLE **5-2c**

Explore the rumor because this is the type of information that HR needs to know. Once you know the truth, make a decision with other managers about what to do. (23)

Category	Number	% of 23	% of Group
Caucasian	12	52	4
African American	7	30	5
Asian	2	9	5
Hispanic	2	9	8

A majority of Caucasian and African American respondents believe it is necessary to disregard the rumor. However, a majority of Hispanic and Asian respondents believe Human Resources should explore the rumor and share the information, if true, with the union.

Typical comments from the Hispanic members of the response group are, "The level of trust in negotiations must be high" and "The integrity of the process must be maintained." Hispanic respondents show consistency in their approach to this dilemma compared with the previous two scenarios: Their belief is that an organization's management must demonstrate honesty and openness in order to be credible. It is interesting to note that Hispanics are less likely than Caucasians or African Americans to be union members in the United States (http://stats.bls.gov).

In the Japanese business culture, individualism is not promoted. A team approach toward meeting organizational needs is, instead, constantly reinforced. Because 96% of the Asian respondents describe themselves as Japanese, this may account for the high percentage of Asians who suggest Human Resources focus on steps that will support the organization as a whole; that is, 73% of Japanese respondents recommend exploring the rumor and advising the union representative if the rumor is accurate.

5-3 Breakdown by Gender

As a point of interest, union membership in the United States is higher among men (15.2%) than among women (11.5%), although the gap has been closing over the last few years (http://stats.bls.gov).

Table 5-3 shows a breakdown by gender.

TABLE **5-3a**

Disregard the rumor—it is only a rumor. (307)

Group	Number	% of 307	% of Group
Male	96	31	58
Female	211	69	60

TABLE **5-3b**

Explore the rumor and advise the union rep what you discover (if true) because the union has probably heard it too—this is good faith bargaining. (177)

Group	Number	% of 177	% of Group
Male	43	24	26
Female	134	76	38

TABLE **5-3c**

Explore the rumor because this is the type of information that HR needs to know. Once you know the truth, make a decision with other managers about what to do. (23)

Group	Number	% of 23	% of Group
Male	20	87	12
Female	3	13	1

There's a nearly equal percentage of each gender that believes the rumor should be disregarded, but the differences surface between men and women who believe the rumor should be explored. Thirty-eight percent of female respondents versus twenty-six percent of male respondents believe that Human Resources should explore the rumor and share the information with the union if it is determined to be accurate. Comments from both men and women in these groups center around building trust between labor and management.

Twelve percent of male respondents, compared to only one percent of female respondents, recommend exploring the rumor because Human Resources should be aware of mergers or acquisitions. A higher percentage of males in this group, then, view themselves as partners with top management and as having a legitimate right to knowledge about potential mergers or acquisitions.

5-4 Breakdown by the Number of Years in Human Resources and Age

Tables 5-4 and 5-5 show breakdowns by number of years in Human Resources and age, respectively.

TABLE **5-4a**

Disregard the rumor—it is only a rumor. (307)

Tenure	Number	% of 307	% of Group
0–1	16	5	18
2–3	30	10	29
4–5	40	13	69
6–10	145	47	82
> 10	76	25	82

TABLE **5-4b**

Explore the rumor and advise the union rep what you discover (if true) because the union has probably heard it too—this is good faith bargaining. (177)

Tenure	Number	% of 177	% of Group
0–1	60	34	67
2–3	64	36	63
4–5	15	8	26
6–10	28	16	16
> 10	10	6	11

TABLE **5-4c**

Explore the rumor because this is the type of information that HR needs to know. Once you discover the truth, make a decision with other managers about what to do. (23)

Tenure	Number	% of 23	% of Group
0–1	4	17	4
2–3	5	22	5
4–5	3	13	5
6–10	3	13	2
> 10	7	30	7.5

TABLE **5-5a**

Disregard the rumor—it is only a rumor. (307)

Age	Number	% of 307	% of Group
<30	46	15	24
31–40	185	60	60
41–50	50	16	83
51–60	26	8	79

TABLE **5-5b**

Explore the rumor and advise the union rep what you discover (if true) because the union has probably heard it too—this is good faith bargaining. (177)

Age	Number	% of 177	% of Group
<30	124	70	65
31–40	43	24	18
41–50	8	5	13
51–60	2	1	6

TABLE **5-5c**

Explore the rumor because this is the type of information that HR needs to know. Once you discover the truth, make a decision with other managers about what to do. (23)

Age	Number	% of 23	% of Group
<30	9	39	5
31–40	6	26	2.5
41–50	2	9	3
51–60	5	22	15

I expected that Human Resource professionals over age 40 would take a more adversarial view of union negotiations and would be less willing to divulge information until it is absolutely necessary. Textbooks on negotiations written prior to the 1990s, such as *Negotiation* by Lewicki and Litterer, address tactics like viewing the other side as "the enemy" and someone not to be trusted.

A majority of respondents with 6-plus years in Human Resources believe the rumor should be totally disregarded. This response group wants to share facts when and only when the facts are shared with Human Resources. Only 24% of respondents under age 30 believe the rumor should be ignored.

Many in the response group under age 30 believe that "good faith bargaining" means proactively exploring the rumor and sharing factual information with the union. In this group of 124 respondents, 53% feel that, if accurate, the rumor should be shared with the union prior to actual negotiations. Of the 10 respondents who are age 41 or older, none wants to share merger information prior to negotiations. They do suggest, however, that Human Resources should wait to disclose at an appropriate time *during* the negotiation process.

Fifteen percent of respondents between ages 51 and 60, compared to 5% of the group under age 30, believe Human Resources should explore the rumor and interject itself into the decision-making process about disclosure. I hoped that survey respondents would perceive themselves as part of the senior management team. The low percentage that see themselves this way may be accounted for by the fact that 68% of the respondents between ages 51 and 60 are at the manager level rather than the director or executive level.

5-5 Breakdown by Organization Type

Table 5-6 shows breakdown by organization type.

TABLE **5-6a**

Disregard the rumor—it is only a rumor. (307)

Type	Number	% of 307	% of Group
Mfg	63	21	67
Svc	96	31	49
NFP	25	8	48
PS	123	40	70

TABLE **5-6b**

Explore the rumor and advise the union rep what you discover (if true) because the union has probably heard it too—this is good faith bargaining. (177)

Type	Number	% of 177	% of Group
Mfg	27	15	29
Svc	90	51	46
NFP	23	13	44
PS	37	21	21

TABLE **5-6c**

Explore the rumor because this is the type of information that HR needs to know. Once you discover the facts, make a decision with other managers about what to do. (23)

Type	Number	% of 23	% of Group
Mfg	4	17	4
Svc	11	48	6
NFP	4	17	8
PS	4	17	2

The two groups with the highest percentage that believe the rumor should be ignored are public sector and manufacturing.

Of the 175 respondents in the public sector, 40% work within the academic community. Typical comments from this response group are, "Time can be spent on more important pursuits" and "When the time is appropriate, executives will share merger or acquisition information. Otherwise, the company could be in violation of **Securities and Exchange Commission (SEC)** regulations."

Another 28% of our public sector respondents work in government agencies, where union membership is higher than in the private sector (http://stats.bls.gov). Themes from this group's comments center on using time (and, thus, taxpayer dollars) wisely and not being driven by countless rumors that run through organizations.

Typical comments from the respondents in the manufacturing response set that argue against disclosure are, "The union already has too much leverage" and "Sharing this information too soon will slow down an already arduous process."

Forty-six percent of service respondents and 44% of nonprofit respondents recommend exploration of the rumor and sharing (factual) discoveries with the union. Over half of the 90 service respondents suggest sharing information prior to the start of formal negotiations. Twelve of the 23 nonprofit respondents make this suggestion. Our service and nonprofit respondents clearly do not project an adversarial stance toward unions. As a follow-up question, members of these two response groups were asked if they had ever worked in a union environment. Seventy-six of the 90 service respondents and 17 of the 23 nonprofit respondents have not worked in a union environment, which may account for their willingness to share information.

Only 8% of the nonprofit respondents and 6% of the service respondents believe the rumor should be explored to enhance HR's knowledge, compared to 4% of manufacturing respondents and 2% of public sector respondents. Many of the nonprofit respondents commented that they work in egalitarian environments in which the Human Resources Manager is perceived as a key member of the management team. Because 31 of the 52 nonprofit organizations represented are also relatively small (500 or fewer employees), this perception that Human Resources should be "in the know" is not surprising.

5-6 Breakdown by Organization Size

Table 5-7 shows the breakdown by organization size.

TABLE **5-7a**

Disregard the rumor—it is only a rumor. (307)

Category	Number	% of 307	% of Group
1	11	4	40
2	40	13	55
3	98	32	62
4	78	25	57
5	80	26	66

TABLE **5-7b**

Explore the rumor and advise the union rep what you discover (if true) because the union has probably heard it too—this is good faith bargaining. (177)

Category	Number	% of 177	% of Group
1	15	5	52
2	29	9	40
3	55	18	35
4	53	17	39
5	25	8	21

TABLE **5-7c**

Explore the rumor because this is the type of information that HR needs to know. Once you know the truth, make a decision with the other managers about what to do. (23)

Category	Number	% of 23	% of Group
1	3	13	10
2	4	15	5
3	5	22	3
4	4	15	3
5	7	30	6

In larger organizations, rumors may prove difficult to source and verify (at least quickly), so my expectation was that fewer respondents in large organizations would recommend taking time to explore a rumor.

Indeed, as the size of company across the response group increases, the percentage that suggests ignoring the rumor also increases. Comments from respondents in companies with 5,001 to 10,000 employees range from, "There's no way I could justify spending time to explore every rumor that surfaces" to "It's not HR's responsibility to pursue the truth to rumors of this nature."

About half of respondents from companies with 100 or fewer employees recommend that Human Resources explore the rumor. The most typical reasons cited for this answer are, "The union rep will hear the rumor, too" and "Why pretend the possibility of a merger doesn't exist when it's common knowledge?" I find it interesting that the reasons provided for sharing information with the union were centered around "common knowledge" rather than in the spirit of building trust.

Chapter Summary

The third ethical dilemma addresses an ever-present scenario in organizations today: controlling rumors. At the beginning of the chapter, I raised three questions related to the ethical implications of this scenario:

1. What role should HR take in sourcing and verifying rumors?
2. How should HR meet the intent as well as the letter of the law in "good faith bargaining"?
3. Can HR balance its roles as protector of management rights and employee advocate given this fact pattern?

Differences occur across demographic groups about the most effective way to address unfounded rumors. As organization size increases across respondents, there is a stronger belief that rumors of this nature should simply be ignored. The two groups with the highest percentage of respondents who believe the rumor should be ignored are public sector and manufacturing respondents. Respondents with more tenure in Human Resource Management and with more years of experience are more likely to suggest that the rumor should be disregarded. With regard to ethnic groups, African American respondents have the lowest percentage who believe that HR should explore the rumor, while Hispanic respondents have the highest percentage.

A majority of all respondents believe HR should not take time to explore rumors that inevitably fly prior to contract bargaining time. One-third of our respondents disagree with this stance and believe that "good faith bargaining" means uncovering and sharing pertinent information. I agree with the one-third minority—I think Human Resources has a responsibility to explore and understand issues that affect the company as a whole *and* its employees.

To be less than forthright in sharing information, Lewicki and Litterer assert in *Negotiation*, results in "deception and disguise" wherein "Each side (the constituency and the opponent) may therefore be played off against the other while the negotiator tries to engineer the agreement he wants most."

None of our survey respondents comments about the ethical implications of balancing HR's obligation to support management with its stewardship role as employee advocate. However, current articles in the Human Resource Management field assert that Human Resource practitioners must be both a strategic partner with management and an employee sponsor or advocate (www. humanresources.about.com/library).

My personal belief is this: if the Human Resources Department does not explore whether the organization may be acquired or involved with a merger, it loses an opportunity to partner with key managers and decide the appropriate time and place to share this information with union representatives.

Discussion Questions

1. Should Human Resources demonstrate loyalty to the company by ignoring the rumor and encouraging employees to do the same?
2. Who would benefit if Human Resources shares information about a pending merger or acquisition?
3. Based on the survey results, do you believe different cultures, age groups, and genders possess different values about sharing information?

Chapter

6

Ethical Dilemma #4: The Boss Wants to Replace Employees with Robots—Should Human Resources Intervene?

Key Terms

Decentralization
Layoffs
Outplacement

Robotics
Strategic planning

Outline

6-1 Breakdown by Total
6-2 Breakdown by Race and Ethnicity
6-3 Breakdown by Number of Years in Human Resources
6-4 Breakdown by Age
6-5 Breakdown by Gender
6-6 Breakdown by Organization Type
6-7 Breakdown by Organization Size
Chapter Summary
Discussion Questions

Robotics *technology has resulted in a robot that can perform a dangerous, skilled labor job within the company. The CEO has indicated that she wants to immediately fire the employees who are currently performing this function and purchase the new technology. Should HR start drawing up the paperwork to terminate these employees or take other steps?*

To be competitive in a global society, many U.S. companies have adopted robotics in their manufacturing process, which often means that employees will be displaced. On the one hand, great strides in technology enable manufacturers to move at a faster, cheaper pace (for more information on robotics, see http://www.robotics.com and http://www.magportal.com). On the other hand, a company can seem cold and indifferent if it lays off its workforce without trying to find alternative ways to use employees' skills.

Human Resources has more than one issue to address in this scenario (Figure 6-1). Certainly, an organization has the right to choose how it

Company Productivity   Employee Rights

Figure 6-1   Balance between individual privacy and company's need to monitor work.

wishes to operate and to determine how many employees are required to meet business objectives. Unless terminations adversely affect a protected segment of the workforce, the company has the legal right to operate with robotics and terminate employees. HR's dilemma is this: Is there a moral obligation to retain employees who have joined the organization, contributed their efforts, and performed effectively?

Another issue is public relations within the community. If a company seemingly fires employees without making an attempt to find other positions for them, will local recruiting be a problem when future needs arise?

Lastly, what is HR's obligation, if any, to step into a situation when the company's top leadership has reached a decision on a course of action? Is HR's role to serve strictly as the enforcer of executive decisions, or should Human Resources at least attempt to become a **strategic planning partner**?

A high percentage of our survey respondents believe that HR should proactively intervene in the decision-making process instead of immediately acting on the CEO's directive.

6-1 Breakdown by Total

Table 6-1 shows a breakdown of responses by total.

TABLE **6-1** Breakdown by Total

HR should proactively intervene	80%
Develop a plan to phase in robotics	22%
Recommend outplacement	32%
Do as the CEO directs	7%
HR's role is communication only	13%
HR should join in the planning process	19%

A majority of our practitioners recommends that HR investigate the feasibility of placing affected employees in other jobs within the company. If retaining employees means that an investment in retraining and reassignment must occur, these respondents feel that HR should recommend this be done. Even if the CEO still decides to terminate the employees, these respondents believe that HR has made a good faith effort to reward employee loyalty and safeguard the company's future recruiting ability.

Of the 415 respondents who believe Human Resources should intervene in the termination decision, 112 suggest that HR investigate the possibility of phasing in the robotics technology. A phase-in approach, they suggest, would allow some overlap between robotics and manual labor.

This approach would provide affected employees with time to locate another position and at the same time ensure that the new technology is viable before the manual process ends.

Almost one-third of our respondents suggest that, regardless of any efforts made to retrain and reassign, HR should recommend an **outplacement** and severance package for employees who lose their jobs. This group feels the company would suffer from negative publicity otherwise and that outplacement is "the right thing to do."

A small percentage (7%) of respondents believes the CEO's plan should be followed as directed, without question. This group of respondents does not address how to counter complaints that the company did not attempt to find a place for affected employees.

Another group of respondents (13%) believes that HR's role should be limited to developing a sound communications plan to inform all employees of the impending **layoffs** and reasons for implementing new technology. They feel that employees will be less angered by the terminations if they understand why the shift to technology must occur. I agree that Human Resources should be involved in this communications process, and I am surprised that such a small percentage of respondents offers this comment.

Only 19% of respondents recommend that Human Resources intervene by attempting to become a part of the planning process. These respondents suggest that HR should meet with the CFO and the CEO and conduct a financial analysis of the impact of robotics and terminating employees, and other viable options for ensuring a safe, productive workplace.

6-2 Breakdown by Race and Ethnicity

I discovered some interesting differences in the approach recommended across the demographic groups, so let's take a look at the breakdown by race and ethnicity shown in Table 6-2.

TABLE **6-2a**

Instead of automatically making preparations to lay off affected employees, investigate the possibility of other jobs within the company—retrain and reassign. (415)

Category	Number	% of 415	% of Group
Caucasian	253	61	80
African American	130	31	96
Asian	20	5	49
Hispanic	12	3	46

TABLE **6-2b**

Investigate the possibility of phasing in the robotics technology and having an overlap between robotics and employees—a phased-in approach. (112)

Category	Number	% of 112	% of Group
Caucasian	80	71	25
African American	5	4	4
Asian	19	17	46
Hispanic	8	7	31

TABLE **6-2c**

Use this change as a PR opportunity to announce that dangerous jobs are being converted so the public doesn't think the company is simply coldhearted. (36)

Category	Number	% of 36	% of Group
Caucasian	10	28	3
African American	17	47	13
Asian	3	8	7
Hispanic	6	17	23

TABLE **6-2d**

Design an outplacement and severance package for affected employees; failure to do so could reflect badly on the company within the community. (163)

Category	Number	% of 163	% of Group
Caucasian	78	48	25
African American	59	36	44
Asian	15	9	37
Hispanic	11	7	42

TABLE **6-2e**

Become a planning partner with CEO/CFO. Conduct a financial analysis of the impact of robotics/layoff of employees, as well as other alternatives to increase the use of technology and have a safe environment. (96)

Category	Number	% of 96	% of Group
Caucasian	47	49	15
African American	29	30	21
Asian	11	11	27
Hispanic	9	9	35

TABLE **6-2f**

Develop a sound communications plan to inform employees of what will occur, and why, and the plan for layoffs. (68)

Category	Number	% of 68	% of Group
Caucasian	38	56	12
African American	14	21	10
Asian	10	15	24
Hispanic	6	9	23

Differences occur across ethnic groups around the degree or level of intervention that is necessary in response to the CEO's directive. For example, almost 100% of the African American respondents believe that Human Resources should proactively intervene by exploring the feasibility of reassigning affected employees, compared to 80% of Caucasian respondents.

I asked some of my African American colleagues how they might account for the high response rate around intervening with the CEO's decision. One theory offered is that within the African American culture, a strong sense of community prevails, perhaps dating back to times in which slavery forced African Americans to serve as one another's sole support system. Another theory offered is that, because of their long history of being on the outside looking in with regard to jobs, African Americans can empathize with a group that is about to become disenfranchised.

Less than one-half of the Asian and Hispanic respondents suggest intervening in a proactive manner. In the Asian business culture, the individual's needs are secondary to the good of the organization, so this finding is expected and tracks with responses to the previous three scenarios from this response group.

Comments from Hispanic respondents who believe their role is to follow the directive revolve around HR trusting the CEO's judgment, unless there is a demonstrated reason not to do so. Elizabeth Scholz, in her article titled "Understanding Foreign Culture Differences" for *Human Resourcer*,[1] summarizes Geert Hofstede's dimensions that differentiate national culture groups. One of these dimensions is power distance, or the degree to which members of the group accept that power throughout their organization is distributed unequally. Mexico, the country from which a high percentage of our respondents have their roots, has a high degree of power distance within its organizations.

---

1. Scholz, Elizabeth. 2000. "Understanding Foreign Culture Differences." *Human Resourcer*, pages 5, 7.

Almost one-half of the Asian respondents recommend intervening by offering a recommendation to phase in robotics and allow employees time to find another position. Less than one-third of Hispanic respondents believe this is the appropriate role for Human Resources. The theme of comments from the Asian respondents centers around protecting the company's ability to recruit employees in the future and not becoming reliant on technology before it is a proven alternative. The theme of comments from the Hispanic respondents centers around an obligation to employees who have been productive and loyal to the company.

Twenty-three percent of Hispanic respondents believe that HR should follow the CEO's directive *but* should design an announcement, for public relations purposes, that explains that dangerous jobs are being converted. This group believes HR must carefully design a communication that shows empathy for those losing their jobs. My Hispanic colleague who advised me about his culture reminded me that many Hispanics can relate to losing a job: Either it is a personal experience or one of a friend or relative.

Only one-fourth of Caucasian respondents suggest that an outplacement and severance package should be designed, as compared to 37% of Asians, 42% of Hispanics, and 44% of African Americans. Many of the Asian and Hispanic respondents are first-generation U.S. citizens, and their cultural norms, which reflect a sense of community and the whole, may still be strong. According to Elizabeth Scholz in her previously mentioned article on cultural differences, the culture within the United States is highly individualistic. People in this culture seek to meet their own interests (and those of their immediate families).

About one-third of Hispanic respondents suggest that HR should attempt to become a planning partner with the CEO and CFO. This high number, considering theoretical support for power distance in the Hispanic culture, may be explained by the fact that many of the respondents are first-generation U.S. citizens. Less than 30% of Asians and African Americans and less than 20% of Caucasians believe that Human Resources should take on this role.

When I speak with Human Resource professionals around the country about developing their role as a strategic planning partner, I often hear wistful comments such as, "If only I *could* have that seat at the Board table." Similar comments were offered on the survey in response to all seven scenarios.

I would like to interject my own comment at this point. As a Human Resource professional, you will not get (or keep) a seat at the Board table unless you have something to say and a way to add value to the executive team. Chapter 10 explores this thought further.

Asians and Hispanics have the largest group percentage that believes HR's role is to follow the CEO's directive and follow up by developing a plan to communicate reasons for the changeover to technology. Over one-third of Hispanics and one-fourth of Asians in our response set are on the other end of the continuum of intervention, so this finding leads me to consider the possibility that respondents' age might affect their belief in the appropriate action.

6-3 Breakdown by Number of Years in Human Resources

Table 6-3 breaks down responses by the number of years in Human Resources.

TABLE **6-3a**

Instead of automatically making preparations to lay off affected employees, investigate the possibility of other jobs within the company—retrain and reassign. (415)

Tenure	Number	% of 415	% of Group
0–1	30	7	34
2–3	95	23	93
4–5	53	13	91
6–10	158	38	90
> 10	79	19	85

TABLE **6-3b**

Investigate the possibility of phasing in the robotics technology and having an overlap between robotics and employees—a phased-in approach. (112)

Tenure	Number	% of 112	% of Group
0–1	1	<1	1
2–3	4	4	4
4–5	10	9	17
6–10	63	56	36
> 10	34	30	37

TABLE **6-3c**

Use this changeover as a PR opportunity to announce that dangerous jobs are being converted so that the public doesn't think the company is simply coldhearted. (36)

Tenure	Number	% of 36	% of Group
0–1	12	33	13
2–3	14	39	14
4–5	2	6	3
6–10	0	0	0
> 10	8	22	9

TABLE **6-3d**

Design an outplacement and severance package for affected employees; failure to do so could reflect badly on the company within the community. (163)

Tenure	Number	% of 163	% of Group
0–1	63	39	71
2–3	74	45	72.5
4–5	4	2	7
6–10	6	4	3
> 10	16	10	17

TABLE **6-3e**

Become a planning partner with the CEO and CFO. Conduct a financial analysis of the impact of robotics/layoff of employees as well as other alternatives to increase the use of technology and have a safe environment. (96)

Tenure	Number	% of 96	% of Group
0–1	0	0	0
2–3	3	3	3
4–5	6	6	10
6–10	48	50	27
> 10	39	41	42

TABLE **6-3f**

Develop a sound communications plan to inform employees of what will occur, and why, and the plan for layoffs. (68)

Tenure	Number	% of 68	% of Group
0–1	27	40	30
2–3	33	49	32
4–5	0	0	0
6–10	1	1	<1
> 10	7	10	7.5

Respondents with Human Resources experience between four and ten years are the most comfortable standing up against the CEO's orders. The younger H.R. practitioners that did *not* recommend countering the directive say they don't have enough position power to take such a proactive and risky stance. Typical comments from this group include, "The CEO wouldn't listen to Human Resources" and "If a top executive has made a decision, H.R. won't have the influence to change it."

6-4 Breakdown by Age

Table 6-4 breaks down responses by age.

TABLE **6-4a**

Instead of automatically making preparations to lay off affected employees, investigate the possibility of other jobs within the company—retrain and reassign. (415)

Age	Number	% of 415	% of Group
<30	125	30	65
31–40	211	51	90
41–50	56	13	93
51–60	23	6	70

TABLE **6-4b**

Investigate the possibility of phasing in the robotics technology and having an overlap between robotics and employees—a phased-in approach. (112)

Age	Number	% of 112	% of Group
<30	5	4	3
31–40	73	65	31
41–50	15	13	25
51–60	19	17	58

T A B L E **6-4c**

Use this changeover as a PR opportunity to announce that dangerous jobs are being converted so that the public doesn't think the company is simply coldhearted. (36)

Age	Number	% of 36	% of Group
<30	26	72	14
31–40	2	6	1
41–50	6	17	10
51–60	2	6	6

T A B L E **6-4d**

Design an outplacement and severance package for affected employees; failure to do so could reflect badly on the company within the community. (163)

Age	Number	% of 163	% of Group
<30	137	84	72
31–40	10	6	4
41–50	11	7	18
51–60	5	3	15

T A B L E **6-4e**

Become a planning partner with the CEO and CFO. Conduct a financial analysis of the impact of robotics/layoff of employees as well as other alternatives to increase the use of technology and have a safe environment. (96)

Age	Number	% of 96	% of Group
<30	3	3	2
31–40	54	56	23
41–50	19	20	32
51–60	20	21	61

T A B L E **6-4f**

Develop a sound communications plan to inform employees of what will occur, and why, and the plan for layoffs. (68)

Age	Number	% of 68	% of Group
<30	60	88	31
31–40	1	1	<1
41–50	4	6	7
51–60	3	4	9

Although a majority of every age group recommends some type of intervention by Human Resources, the cohort between ages 41–50 has the largest group percentage that believes Human Resources should counter the CEO's directive with a recommendation to retrain and reassign. Ninety percent of 31–40-year-olds make this recommendation.

Respondents in the 51–60 age group that do not believe Human Resources should go against the CEO's directive make comments such as, "HR should pick battles it can win" and "I must carry out the boss's directive or I may be next to go." That's a world-weary, defeated attitude. What a shame.

Over half of the 51–60-year-old respondents, however, would advise a phase-in approach to protect the company from moving too quickly into using technology that may not work. This more tenured group of respondents suggests that alternatives almost always exist to a blanket layoff, and HR's role is to develop and offer those alternatives.

Fourteen percent of respondents under age 30 suggest Human Resources should follow the CEO's directive but also develop a public relations announcement. This group feels that the company's image in the community will affect its ability to recruit in the future. Zemke, Raines, and Filipczak, in *Generations At Work*,[2] find that Generation Xers are very conscious of a company's image within the community and this image is a factor in their decision whether to take a position with the company. Seventy-two percent of our respondents under age 30 suggest that a PR-conscious company should design an outplacement and severance package for affected employees, compared to 15% of 51–60-year-old respondents. Nearly one-third of the under age 30 respondents recommends development of a sound communications plan, as opposed to only 9% of respondents between the ages of 51–60.

I expected that older, more tenured respondents might recommend that Human Resources attempt to become a planning partner with the CEO and CFO. These respondents, I thought, would be more secure in their ability, expertise, and right to have access to information that top executives have with regard to the company's future. Indeed, as the respondents' age increases, so does the likelihood they will take this approach. Almost one-third (32%) of respondents between ages 41–50 and 61% of those between 51–60 suggest becoming a planning partner.

---

2. Zemke, Raines, and Filipczak, *Generations At Work*, page 248.

6-5 Breakdown by Gender

Table 6-5 breaks down responses by gender.

T A B L E **6-5a**

Instead of automatically making preparations to lay off affected employees, investigate the possibility of other jobs within the company—retrain and reassign. (415)

Group	Number	% of 415	% of Group
Male	110	27	66
Female	305	73	87

T A B L E **6-5b**

Investigate the possibility of phasing in the robotics technology and having an overlap between robotics and employees—phased-in approach. (112)

Group	Number	% of 112	% of Group
Male	57	51	34
Female	55	49	16

T A B L E **6-5c**

Use this changeover as a PR opportunity to announce that dangerous jobs are being converted so that the public doesn't think the company is simply coldhearted. (36)

Group	Number	% of 36	% of Group
Male	9	25	5
Female	27	75	8

T A B L E **6-5d**

Design an outplacement and severance package for affected employees; failure to do so could reflect badly on the company within the community. (163)

Group	Number	% of 163	% of Group
Male	67	41	40
Female	96	59	27

TABLE **6-5e**

Become a planning partner with the CEO and CFO. Conduct a financial analysis of the impact of robotics/layoff of employees and other alternatives to increase use of technology and provide a safe environment. (96)

Group	Number	% of 96	% of Group
Male	54	56	32.5
Female	42	44	12

TABLE **6-5f**

Develop a sound communications plan to inform employees of what will occur, and why, and the plan for layoffs. (68)

Group	Number	% of 68	% of Group
Male	17	25	10
Female	51	75	14

In their responses, more men are company-centered and more women are employee-centered.

A slightly higher percentage of women than men suggests the importance of a sound communications plan for employees. Researchers Deborah Tannen *(You Just Don't Understand)*[3] and Glaser and Smalley *(Swim With the Dolphins)*[4] assert that women in the workplace are more nurturing and empathic than their male counterparts. I expected then, that female respondents would be more likely than men to recommend ways to act on behalf of those employees in danger of losing their jobs.

A majority of female respondents believe that HR should not react by immediately terminating employees, compared to 66% of male respondents. The central theme of comments made by these women is around standing up for the employees' rights, while most of the men's comments revolve around not acting hastily in a way that could damage the company. Just over one-third of male respondents believe HR's role is to investigate a phase-in approach, while only 16% of female respondents make this recommendation.

More men (40%) than women (27%) suggest development of an out-placement and severance package. The men's comments in this response set centered around minimizing chances of a negative image in the community, while the women's comments were more focused on advocacy for

---

3. Tannen, Deborah. 1990. *You Just Don't Understand.* William Morrow and Company, Inc., page 25.

4. Glaser and Smalley, *Swim With the Dolphins*, page 206.

individuals. I believe that both concerns are valid! Individuals who are not treated well go into the community and talk about their experiences within the workplace.

One-third of men compared to 12% of women recommend joining with the CEO or CFO to conduct a financial analysis of options available to the company. I thought this gender difference in the response rate might be related to the position/level of respondents. However, when I revisited that factor, I found that the women in this 12% are primarily at Vice President or Director level—a level that I consider strategic.

6-6 Breakdown by Organization Type

Table 6-6 breaks down responses by organization type.

TABLE **6-6a**

Instead of automatically making preparations to lay off affected employees, investigate the possibility of other jobs within the company—retrain and reassign. (415)

Type	Number	% of 415	% of Group
Mfg	70	17	74
Svc	190	46	96
NFP	26	6	50
PS	129	31	74

TABLE **6-6b**

Investigate the possibility of phasing in robotics technology and having an overlap between robotics and employees—a phased-in approach. (112)

Type	Number	% of 112	% of Group
Mfg	34	30	36
Svc	6	5	3
NFP	26	23	50
PS	46	41	26

TABLE **6-6c**

Use this changeover as a PR opportunity to announce that dangerous jobs are being converted so that the public doesn't think the company is simply coldhearted. (36)

Type	Number	% of 36	% of Group
Mfg	11	31	12
Svc	6	17	3
NFP	5	14	10
PS	14	39	8

TABLE **6-6d**

Design an outplacement and severance package for affected employees; failure to do so could reflect badly on company within the community. (163)

Type	Number	% of 163	% of Group
Mfg	57	35	61
Svc	30	18	15
NFP	7	4	13
PS	69	42	39

TABLE **6-6e**

Become a planning partner with the CEO/CFO. Conduct a financial analysis of the impact of robotics/layoff of employees and other alternatives to increase use of technology and provide a safe environment. (96)

Type	Number	% of 96	% of Group
Mfg	13	14	14
Svc	49	51	25
NFP	3	3	6
PS	31	32	18

TABLE **6-6f**

Develop a sound communications plan to inform employees about what will occur, and why, and the plan for layoffs. (68)

Type	Number	% of 68	% of Group
Mfg	4	6	4
Svc	18	26	9
NFP	8	12	15
PS	38	56	22

Nearly 100% of service company respondents want to explore the feasibility of retraining and reassigning employees! The percentage of public sector and manufacturing respondents who make this suggestion is the same (74%), and 50% of nonprofit respondents choose this course. I was pleasantly surprised by the high percentage of public sector respondents that do not recommend merely reacting to the CEO's edict. In *The New Institutionalism in Organizational Analysis*,[5] Scott and Meyer offer their

---

5. Scott, Richard and Meyer, John W. "The Organization of Societal Sectors: Propositions and Early Evidence," *The New Institutionalism in Organizational Analysis*, W. Powell and P. DiMaggio, eds. Chicago: The University of Chicago Press, pages 129–137.

findings that public sector organizations typically engage in centralized decision making (as opposed to **decentralized** decision making in service organizations). Decisions are made at the top levels and directors and midmanagers are expected to carry them out, without question. Scott and Meyer's findings track with my own experiences in public sector organizations. I take the current (different) mindset as a good sign.

Forty of the 70 manufacturing respondents comment that employees are likely to be union members and, as such, have some protection from immediate layoff. Seventy-five of the 190 service respondents comment that their ability to find qualified employees is limited, and terminating employees without searching for potential openings within the company is a poor business decision. The remaining 115 service respondents feel that the company should express some loyalty to its employees and make a good faith effort to retrain and reassign.

A significant percentage of manufacturing respondents recommends an outplacement and severance package for affected employees, compared to 39% for public sector respondents and only 15% of service and 13% of nonprofit respondents. Most of the manufacturing respondents, many of whom represent union companies, comment that they are concerned that displaced employees be treated fairly.

One-fourth of the service respondents recommends that Human Resources become a planning partner with the CEO. Because service organizations are more likely than the other types of organizations represented to engage in decentralized decision making, I was not surprised that just 18% of public sector, 14% of manufacturing, and 6% of nonprofit respondents provide this recommendation.

Almost one-fourth of public sector respondents believe Human Resources should develop a sound communications strategy, and that should be the limitation of its role. *Each* of the 38 people with this recommendation asserts that it is the organization's duty to ensure that employees understand the business reasons for lost jobs so they don't think their lack of competence caused the termination. I agree: I just don't think HR should stop with being the messenger, and *just* the messenger.

6-7 Breakdown by Organization Size

Table 6-7 breaks down responses by organization size.

TABLE **6-7a**

Instead of automatically making preparations to lay off affected employees, investigate the possibility of other jobs within the company—retrain and reassign. (415)

Category	Number	% of 415	% of Group
1	16	4	55
2	39	9	53
3	137	33	86
4	114	27	84
5	109	26	90

TABLE **6-7b**

Investigate the possibility of phasing in robotics technology and having an overlap between robotics and employees—a phased-in approach. (112)

Category	Number	% of 112	% of Group
1	13	12	45
2	43	38	59
3	22	20	14
4	22	20	16
5	12	11	10

TABLE **6-7c**

Use this changeover as a PR opportunity to announce that dangerous jobs are being converted so the public doesn't think the company is simply coldhearted. (36)

Category	Number	% of 36	% of Group
1	5	14	17
2	12	33	16
3	8	22	5
4	6	17	4
5	3	8	2

TABLE **6-7d**

Design an outplacement and severance package for affected employees; failure to do so could reflect badly on the company within the community. (163)

Category	Number	% of 163	% of Group
1	2	1	7
2	15	9	20.5
3	31	19	19
4	47	29	35
5	68	42	56

TABLE **6-7e**

Become a planning partner with the CEO and CFO. Conduct a financial analysis of the impact of robotics/layoff of employees as well as other alternatives to increase use of technology and provide a safe environment. (96)

Category	Number	% of 96	% of Group
1	11	11	38
2	37	39	51
3	24	25	15
4	17	18	12.5
5	7	7	6

TABLE **6-7f**

Develop a sound communications plan to inform employees of what will occur, and why, and the plan for layoffs. (68)

Category	Number	% of 68	% of Group
1	6	9	21
2	0	0	0
3	9	13	6
4	22	32	16
5	31	46	26

In large organizations, Human Resources may be far removed, geographically speaking, from the workforce. One might expect that carrying out a directive to terminate a certain segment of the employee population would be easier for HR because of this depersonalized setting.

The opposite holds true in our response set! Ninety percent of the respondents in companies with 5,001–10,000 employees believe Human Resources should investigate opportunities to retrain and reassign. The percentage is likewise high for respondents in companies with 1,001–5,000 employees (84%) and in companies with 501–1,000 employees (86%). Comments made most often by respondents in these three categories are, "Surely, positions can be found within the company," "It's too difficult to find quality employees, so keep these workers," and "Human Resources needs to be an advocate for the employees and save the company from losing quality people."

Forty-nine percent of respondents from companies with 101–500 employees would follow the directive of the CEO but would recommend a phase-in approach. The reason most often offered for this answer is that jobs within the company may be limited, and HR's role should be to ensure a smooth transition between robotics and manual labor so productivity will not be affected.

I was surprised that only 36 respondents note a concern that this action might be viewed negatively in the community, and almost half of these respondents are from companies with 500 or fewer employees. Many in this group of 36 noted a public relations concern—the potential impact of a layoff on future recruiting efforts.

Over half of respondents from the largest companies (5,001–10,000 employees) believe HR's role is to recommend an outplacement package. Just 7% of respondents from the smallest companies (100 or less) recommend this action. Smaller companies may simply not have the financial resources to offer outplacement, which may account for so few in this group making this recommendation.

Our smaller company representatives are more likely than other respondents to perceive themselves as strategic planning partners with top executives. Over half of the respondents from companies with 101–500 employees and over one-third of respondents from companies with 100 or less employees believe HR's role is to try to become a planning partner. With a hierarchical structure to contend with in larger companies, it is feasible that junior and mid-level Human Resource practitioners do not encounter opportunities to work closely with those at an executive level. Only 138 of our 518 respondents has a Vice President title, so the number that may interact with the CEO or CFO on a regular basis is limited.

Chapter Summary

The ethical dilemma faced in this scenario revolves around replacing loyal employees with technology. Three important issues are raised:

- Does HR have a moral obligation to urge a company to retain employees who have loyally served the organization?
- Should HR consider the public relations impact of laying off employees in favor of technology?
- What is HR's role, if any, beyond enforcement of the leadership's decisions?

Overwhelmingly, our respondents feel that a company in this position *does* have a moral obligation to at least attempt to retrain and reassign employees. To a lesser extent, public relations within the community is a consideration, especially for smaller organizations that may have difficulty recruiting employees. I agree with our respondents: I see a moral obligation to at least help employees become employable even though we cannot guarantee lifetime employment.

There are some notable differences across demographic groups. For example, more men than women recommend a phased-in approach toward adding robotics and an outplacement package for employees who will be replaced with technology. Larger companies and manufacturing sector organizations are most likely to recommend outplacement. Smaller company representatives are most likely to view HR's role as a facilitator for the smooth transition between people and robotics as the production methodology. Organizations in the service sector are most likely to recommend that HR's role is to explore retraining and retaining affected employees.

Only a small percentage of respondents believe that Human Resources should move beyond serving as an enforcer of leadership's directives to seek the role of strategic planning partner. I encourage Human Resource professionals to become more involved in transitions such as the move to robotics. At the very least, Human Resources should consider techniques to ease employees into the transition by providing information about impending changes and offering counseling about the importance of learning new skills. In the new millennium, I hope that more HR practitioners will expand their role by taking a stand and proactively sharing their views and values with top leadership.

Discussion Questions

1. Should community image be a driving factor in a company's decision to terminate a large group of employees? If not, what should be the driving factor?
2. In an "at-will" state, (where organizations can fire employees without notice) what is an organization's moral contract with employees?
3. Does a Human Resources practitioner have the right to interfere with an organization's business decisions, once they have been made?

Ethical Dilemma #5: How Much "Truth" Should Recruiters Disclose to Applicants?

Key Terms

Baby boomers	Generation Xers	Radio babies

Outline

7-1 Breakdown by Total
7-2 Breakdown by Race and Ethnicity
7-3 Breakdown by Gender
7-4 Breakdown by Number of Years in Human Resources and Age
7-5 Breakdown by Organization Type
7-6 Breakdown by Organization Size
Chapter Summary
Discussion Questions

Recruiting for all positions within your organization has become very challenging. You are tempted when you are interviewing to assure potential employees that your company is financially stable, with little fluctuation in staffing and no organizational changes planned that will affect job descriptions. This may or may not be the case, because the company has experienced many changes in leadership and policies over the past 2 years. However, you have no current knowledge of instability or projected changes. What is your obligation to potential employees?

Recruiting and retaining a quality workforce are critical challenges in the new millennium, and the competition to hire the best and the brightest is keen. Given this competitive environment, one line of thinking is that it would be foolhardy to warn applicants of potential organizational instability. On the other hand, some might think Human Resources is obligated to disclose the company's true business situation so that applicants can make an informed decision. I believe, as do the authors of *Human Resources Management,* 7th edition, that a company's public relations opportunities can be enhanced with open, honest communication during the recruiting process. Dishonesty in the recruiting process can result in a decidedly negative perception of the organization within the community.[1]

7-1 Breakdown by Total

Table 7-1 breaks down responses by total.

T A B L E **7-1** Breakdown by Total

Tell applicants about pending changes	79%
Share long-term objectives with applicants	19%
Share only known facts with applicants	16%

---

1. *Human Resources Management,* page 207.

The overwhelming response to this ethical dilemma is to tell applicants about the changes and potential instability of the company! Seventy-nine percent believes Human Resources should explain situational dynamics to applicants because the company's reputation in the community might be jeopardized if people are not provided with the facts.

Of the 407 respondents who recommend disclosure of both the company's past changes and potential changes, 100 suggest that Human Resources share the company's long-term objectives and goals and how the job openings fit into the planning process. Research by Zemke, Raines, and Filipczak *(Generations At Work)*,[2] as well as research I conducted in 1999 and 2000, finds that **Generation Xers,** in particular, want to understand their role in carrying out an organization's strategic plan, so this course of action would likely appeal to applicants in this age group.

Less than one-fifth of our respondents believe Human Resources' responsibility is to share only the known facts about the company's plans and activities. To this group, divulging any additional information without an applicant's direct question constitutes disloyalty to the company. These respondents suggest that hiring managers can elect to speculate, if they choose to do so, about the company's stability.

7-2 Breakdown by Race and Ethnicity

As with the previous scenarios, some differences emerge across demographic groups. Let's start with a breakdown by race and ethnicity, shown in Table 7-2.

TABLE **7-2a**

Tell the truth—tell applicants about the changing dynamics. (407)

Category	Number	% of 407	% of Group
Caucasian	249	61	79
African American	114	28	84
Asian	30	7	73
Hispanic	14	3	54

---

2. Zemke, Raines, and Filipczak, *Generations At Work*, page 82.

TABLE **7-2b**

Share the company's long-term plans with candidates and explain their role in helping the company achieve those plans. (100)

Category	Number	% of 100	% of Group
Caucasian	46	46	15
African American	39	39	29
Asian	10	10	24
Hispanic	5	5	19

TABLE **7-2c**

Share only the facts you know for certain. Let hiring managers discuss the changing environment if they choose to do so. (84)

Category	Number	% of 84	% of Group
Caucasian	68	81	21.5
African American	7	8	5
Asian	6	7	15
Hispanic	3	4	11.5

I expected to find that Asian respondents would demonstrate loyalty toward the company and would be less inclined to share potentially negative information with applicants. In the Asian culture, there is a strong belief that a mistake is something to be ashamed of, and mistakes are often denied or buried (http://goldsea.com). I also expected that the comments from Hispanic and African American respondents would be oriented toward sharing information with individual applicants, based on input my Hispanic and African American colleagues provided about their respective cultures. Their sense of community, my colleagues suggest, would lead them to provide information about the company to potential employees.

Eighty-four percent of African American respondents recommend being forthright with applicants, followed by 79% of Caucasians and 73% of Asians. Just over half (54%) of Hispanics recommend this approach, which is a lower percentage (compared to those other three groups) than I expected, based on Hispanic respondents' comments in the previous scenarios about being open.

Less than one-third of African American respondents suggest sharing the company's strategic objectives with applicants. Almost one-fourth of Asian respondents makes this recommendation, although I expected a higher percentage because of the Asian business concept of individuals supporting the whole. A common theme throughout the comments from these two groups is that individuals can more effectively support the whole organization if they are well informed. I strongly agree with this belief—I have found that organizational commitment is highly correlated with individuals' understanding of their role in supporting organizational objectives.

Caucasian respondents have the highest group percentage that recommends sharing only the known facts with applicants. The central theme from comments made by these respondents is protection of company interests. They want to secure applicants' commitment as employees before "sharing dirty laundry."

7-3 Breakdown by Gender

Table 7-3 breaks down responses by gender.

TABLE **7-3a**

Tell the truth—tell applicants about the changing dynamics. (407)

Group	Number	% of 407	% of Group
Male	97	24	58
Female	310	76	88

TABLE **7-3b**

Share the company's long-term plans with candidates and explain their role in helping the company achieve those plans. (100)

Group	Number	% of 100	% of Group
Male	22	22	13
Female	78	78	22

TABLE **7-3c**

Share only the facts you know for certain. Let hiring managers discuss the changing environment if they choose to do so. (84)

Group	Number	% of 84	% of Group
Male	52	62	31
Female	32	38	9

There are marked differences in how men and women in the survey would handle this situation! Women in our response group are more willing to forge a partnership with applicants, while men in the response group are more likely to forge their alliance with the company.

Previous research led me to believe that I would encounter differences in the way men and women would address the current and other ethical dilemmas posed in the survey. Carol Gilligan published a significant study in 1982 that even today is the source of dialogue about gender differences in the workplace: *In a Different Voice* (www.facstaff.bucknell.edu).[3] A former colleague of Kohlberg, Gilligan challenges his stage theory of moral development and asserts that a feminine construction of reality exists. Carol Gilligan suggests that women's self-perception is closely connected with relationships with others.

Almost 90% of female respondents recommend discussing potential organizational instability, compared to 58% of male respondents. Typical comments from women are, "Applicants have a right to know what they're getting into" and "People should have the right information they need to make a decision." The main theme that surfaced from the men's responses is around retention. They warn that when people find out that the company is volatile, they will feel betrayed and will leave for a more stable environment.

More men than women suggest sharing the company's long-term objectives with applicants. The reasoning most often given by both men and women for this approach is that applicants can readily understand where their skills and expertise fit into the company's plans. Female respondents most often use language such as, "We want to build a team, with applicants understanding their role in the company's success." Men in this group assert that fairness dictates sharing the company's strategy, short of sharing proprietary information.

---

3. Gilligan, Carol. 1993. *In a Different Voice: Psychological Theory and Women's Development.* Cambridge, MA: Harvard University Press.

7-4 Breakdown by Number of Years in Human Resources and Age

Table 7-4 breaks down responses by the number of years in Human Resources; Table 7-5 shows response breakdowns by age.

T A B L E **7-4a**

Tell the truth—tell applicants about the changing dynamics. (407)

Tenure	Number	% of 407	% of Group
0–1	70	17	79
2–3	66	16	65
4–5	44	11	76
6–10	137	34	78
>10	90	22	97

T A B L E **7-4b**

Share the company's long-term plans with candidates and explain their role in helping the company. (100)

Tenure	Number	% of 100	% of Group
0–1	60	60	67
2–3	31	31	30
4–5	6	6	10
6–10	3	3	2
>10	0	0	0

T A B L E **7-4c**

Share only the facts you know for certain. Let hiring managers discuss the changing environment if they choose to do so. (84)

Tenure	Number	% of 84	% of Group
0–1	14	17	16
2–3	29	35	28
4–5	10	12	17
6–10	28	33	16
>10	3	4	3

TABLE **7-5a**

Tell the truth—tell applicants about the changing dynamics. (407)

Age	Number	% of 407	% of Group
<30	136	33	71
31–40	181	44	77
41–50	58	14	97
51–60	32	8	97

TABLE **7-5b**

Share the company's long-term plans with candidates and explain their role in helping the company achieve those plans. (100)

Age	Number	% of 100	% of Group
<30	91	91	48
31–40	9	9	4
41–50	0	0	0
51–60	0	0	0

TABLE **7-5c**

Share only the facts you know for certain. Let hiring managers discuss changing environment if they choose to do so. (84)

Age	Number	% of 84	% of Group
<30	43	51	22.5
31–40	38	45	16
41–50	3	4	5
51–60	0	0	0

I anticipated different responses based on age because of research I conducted recently on generation differences in the workplace. In 1999 and 2000, I interviewed 500 people in each of four age groups working in organizations around the United States. One of the questions I asked was: "What entices you to join an organization?" The answer was different for each age group interviewed:

- People born between 1930–1945 radio
- People born between 1946–1964 baby
- People born between 1965–1976 X
- People born between 1977–1985 Y

Generation Xers, those born between 1965–1976, overwhelmingly responded to this question by saying that alignment with a recruiting company's mission and vision, and the ability to balance work and family life, were critical factors in their decision to take a position (and stay with) a company.

Baby boomers, people born between 1946–1964, typically said they were drawn to companies where they could transfer their retirement package or that had an excellent benefit program for transition years.

Radio babies, those born between 1930–1945, said that they had no intention of leaving their present company because they were ready to retire (or had retired and been hired back as consultants). They indicated, however, that when they had been looking for a position, the features they looked for were a good salary and company stability.

People from Generation Y, the generation just coming out of high school and college, most often commented that they wanted to start their own companies if they could not find a position that offers a good salary, work-life balance, and the chance to make a difference in the world.

I expected, based on this research, that Generation Xers would feel that Human Resources should be candid with applicants about the company's ups and downs. Generation Xers watched as their parents or friends' parents were downsized in the mid-1980s and early 1990s, after years of loyalty to their company. After witnessing this, I predicted that Generation Xers in our response set would be cautious—and expect their peers to be cautious—regarding the selection of which organization to join.

Ninety-seven percent of respondents with over 10 years' experience (most of whom are the youngest Baby boomers or oldest Generation Xers) believe candor is the right course, compared to 79% of respondents with 1 year or less in the field. A very high percentage (92%) within the more seasoned group suggests that the company's ability to recruit over the long term will be affected by how it handles this sensitive situation. Experience is a good teacher.

Almost half of our respondents under age 30 believe Human Resources should share the company's long-term objectives, while 22.5% of this group wants Human Resources to share only known facts with applicants (compared to zero respondents in the 51–60 age group). The reason most often given for only sharing known facts is that projecting what might occur in the future is the purview of hiring managers. I believe Human Resource professionals must move out of this box and use our experience, expertise, and research to make—and share—our predictions for the future!

7-5 Breakdown by Organization Type

Table 7-6 breaks down responses by organization type.

TABLE **7-6a**

Tell the truth—tell applicants about the changing dynamics. (407)

Type	Number	% of 407	% of Group
Mfg	47	12	50
Svc	177	43	90
NFP	29	7	56
PS	154	38	88

TABLE **7-6b**

Share the company's long-term plans with candidates and explain their role in helping the company achieve those plans. (100)

Type	Number	% of 100	% of Group
Mfg	13	13	14
Svc	71	71	36
NFP	3	3	6
PS	13	13	7

TABLE **7-6c**

Share only the facts you know for certain. Let hiring managers discuss the changing environment if they choose to do so. (84)

Type	Number	% of 84	% of Group
Mfg	29	35	31
Svc	18	21	9
NFP	20	24	38
PS	17	20	10

The majority of service and public sector respondents believe it is necessary to advise applicants of the company's changing dynamics. The most typical comment among service company respondents is, "An organization's ability to recruit in the future hinges on how truthful Human Resources is to current applicants." Comments from public sector respondents had a primary theme: Telling the truth to potential applicants is simply the right thing to do. Recruiting in the public sector arena is often difficult because salaries often cannot compete with those of the private sector, so I was pleasantly surprised to find that such a high percentage of these respondents is willing to sacrifice potential recruits in the interest of openness.

Over one-third of service company respondents believes Human Resources should share long-term company plans with candidates, compared to 14% of manufacturing, 7% of public sector, and 6% of nonprofit respondents. This tracks with previous research I conducted in 2000. A survey of 5,000 organizations across the United States revealed that 62% of the service organizations, 31% of the manufacturing organizations, 20% of public sector organizations, and 18% of nonprofits conduct strategic planning. I believe that a strategic plan must be in place, and Human Resources must be privy to it, before sharing with applicants can be even considered as an option.

Thirty-eight percent of the nonprofit and 31% of manufacturing respondents believe HR's role is to only share facts with applicants and let hiring managers discuss the changing environment. Most of the people in these two response groups did not say they would push for the hiring managers to disclose information: Less than 5% in each of the two groups indicated they would proactively recommend this tactic to hiring managers.

7-6 Breakdown by Organization Size

Table 7-7 breaks down responses by organization size.

TABLE **7-7a**

Tell the truth—tell applicants about the changing dynamics. (407)

Category	Number	% of 407	% of Group
1	15	4	52
2	52	13	71
3	131	32	82
4	111	27	82
5	98	24	81

TABLE **7-7b**

Share the company's long-term plans with candidates and explain their role in helping the company achieve those plans. (100)

Category	Number	% of 100	% of Group
1	16	16	55
2	33	33	45
3	14	14	9
4	18	18	13
5	9	9	7

TABLE **7-7c**

Share only the facts you know for certain. Let hiring managers discuss changing environment if they choose to do so. (84)

Category	Number	% of 84	% of Group
1	14	17	48
2	19	23	26
3	28	33	18
4	16	19	12
5	7	8	6

Human Resources may not have access to information about the changing dynamics in larger organizations (or at least not quickly), so I expected that the representatives from large companies would not be as likely to recommend sharing information with applicants as are those from small companies.

Actually, responses from companies in categories 3, 4, and 5 are very close with regard to being in favor of sharing information about the company's changing dynamics. A common theme from respondents in these groups is the importance of preserving the company's reputation for having integrity within the community.

Fifty-five percent of respondents from the smallest companies (100 or fewer employees) suggest that HR's role is to share the company's long-term plans, as compared to only 7% of those from 5,001–10,000 employee companies. Because the top leadership of large companies is generally removed in geographic distance or hierarchy from Human Resources, this is the response I expected. *My hope, however, is to see a trend over the next few years in which Human Resource practitioners in companies of all sizes proactively solicit information about long-term objectives and their role in meeting those objectives.*

Almost half of the category 1 respondents believe Human Resources should share only facts with applicants and defer to the hiring managers to decide what additional information should be passed along. A large percentage of Human Resource practitioners (90%) in the smallest companies represented serve primarily in an administrative role (such as screening, benefits administration, orientation) and indicated discomfort with stepping outside that role.

Chapter Summary

The dilemma facing Human Resources in this scenario is how to balance the rights of applicants to understand the type of company they may be hired to work for with the company's need to quickly fill open positions in a competitive marketplace.

Across survey respondents, the overwhelming response is that Human Resources should share information about the company's changing dynamics with applicants. The primary impetus behind this response is that the company's reputation within the community must be safeguarded to ensure future recruiting capability. Less than 20% of respondents suggest deferring disclosure of this type of information to hiring managers.

There are differences in the degree of sharing, and reasons provided for sharing, across demographic groups. Women in the response set are more likely to lean toward building a partnership with applicants and men are more apt to partner with the company to protect its interests. We will see this different reasoning between genders in later scenarios discussed in this book. Older survey respondents are more likely to believe the disclosure of information is best left to the hiring manager's discretion, while Generation Xers believe Human Resources should provide information to the fullest extent possible. Service and public sector organization respondents are more willing to open up to applicants, and smaller company respondents are more likely than those from larger companies to share the organization's long-term objectives.

Discussion Questions

1. Given a choice, do you think it is more important for an organization to be perceived as open within its local community or hold information about its mistakes and changing dynamics "close to the vest"?
2. If a company's top leadership does not share impending changes with Human Resources, is it HR's responsibility to proactively seek information that affects the department's capacity to recruit and retain employees?

Chapter

8

Ethical Dilemma #6: Monitoring Technology for Telecommuters Is Available, But Should It Be Used?

Key Terms

Fair Labor Standards Act (FLSA)   Telecommuting

Outline

8-1 Breakdown by Total
8-2 Breakdown by Race and Ethnicity
8-3 Breakdown by Gender
8-4 Breakdown by Number of Years in Human Resources and Age
8-5 Breakdown by Organization Type
8-6 Breakdown by Organization Size
Chapter Summary
Discussion Questions

Several employees within your organization have received permission to telecommute. Their managers are concerned that productivity may suffer because employees will not have direct supervision when they are working at home. Should you recommend technology that monitors log-in and log-out times, keystrokes, and sites they access on the Internet during work hours?

"New forms of work and organization are forming in cyberspace, making many traditional jobs and skills obsolete. This phenomenon has been named the virtual organization."[1]

A 1999 study titled *Nothing But Net*,[2] conducted by Rutgers University Center for Survey Research and Analysis, found that 41% of workers said that they could do their job from a remote location provided they were given the proper technology. Only 16% of those interviewed said that their employers were willing to offer the option to work at home! Studies such as this, and my own conversations with managers across the country, show that companies are wary of trusting employees to work off site.

To complicate matters, there is no shortage of electronic monitoring systems available that managers can access for surveillance purposes, according to *Workplace Visions* (Number 3, 2000).[3] Some of these systems include:

- Internet Manager   Software that scans for and identifies "cyber-loafers" and notifies employees that they are being monitored each time they log onto the Internet.

---

1. Crandall, N. Frederic, Ph.D., and Wallace, Marc J., Jr., Ph.D. 1998. *Work and Rewards in the Virtual Workplace.* Center for Workforce Effectiveness, pages 4, 51.

2. Rutgers University Center for Survey Research and Analysis. 1999. *Nothing But Net.*

3. "How Will New Technologies Change the Human Resource Management Profession?" 2000. *Workplace Visions,* Number 3, page 4.

Figure 8-1   The dilemma.

- Investigator   Software that captures all the keystrokes typed into a computer, including keystrokes an employee may delete.
- Super Scout   Software that automatically filters and sorts every word that enters through a network.

On the one hand, computer technology has greatly enhanced our productive capacity over the last 20 years, and breakthroughs in the field are occurring on a regular basis. Computer technology affords organizations the opportunity to establish **telecommuting** programs that appeal to employees who are attempting to minimize the stress of daily commutes to and from the office. On the other hand, privacy was one of the hottest workplace issues debated throughout the 1990s, and several professional organizations have actively opposed the monitoring of employee communications such as e-mail, according to Peggy Smith and Jean Hanebury in *Issues in the Workplace: Human Resource Dilemmas*.[4]

The dilemma presented here addresses whether HR's role is to protect employee privacy or monitor the use of company resources—employees' time and computers (Figure 8-1).

---

4. Smith, P., and Hanebury, J. 2000. *Issues in the Workplace: Human Resource Dilemmas*. Cincinnati, OH: South-Western Publishing, page 12.

8-1 Breakdown by Total

Table 8-1 breaks down responses by total.

TABLE **8-1**   Breakdown by Total

Do not recommend technology	55%
Recommend technology	45%
HR should develop telecommuting guidelines	20%
HR should design face time for telecommuters	4%
Monitor results, not process	30%

Just over half of the respondents believe that Human Resources should *not* recommend technology that closely monitors employee activities. The primary theme across this group is that an organization must trust its employees to promote people taking responsibility for their work. If the company is effective in its selection of employees in the first instance, and chooses appropriate people to participate in the telecommuting program, the issue of trust should not be a consideration according to this group of respondents.

Twenty percent of the group that is against monitoring suggest that HR's role is to manage the telecommuting process by getting to know potential telecommuters and providing guidance on working in a home office. I applaud these few who believe in treating employees as individuals!

Only a small percentage of the population suggests development of opportunities for telecommuters to have "face time" in the office on a regular basis. Their rationale for this suggestion is that visible telecommuters will still remain a part of the office landscape and will not be left out of key decisions and activities.

Almost one-third of respondents believe that Human Resources should recommend that supervisors monitor results, rather than process. They suggest that the objective should be for telecommuters to complete assignments on time in a quality manner, not to monitor whether they might take a few minutes during the work day to surf the Net.

Forty-five percent of respondents believe that Human Resources *should* recommend technology to closely monitor telecommuters. Of this group, 160 respondents suggest that the role of Human Resources is to ensure that employees are productive, in order to protect the company's interests. They assert that employees should understand that being monitored electronically is a trade-off for the opportunity to work at home.

8-2 Breakdown by Race and Ethnicity

Table 8-2 breaks down responses by race and ethnicity.

T A B L E **8-2a**

Do not recommend monitoring technology. (287)

Category	Number	% of 287	% of Group
Caucasian	152	53	48
African American	79	27.5	58.5
Asian	36	12.5	88
Hispanic	20	7	77

T A B L E **8-2b**

Work on building trust with telecommuting employees. (105)

Category	Number	% of 105	% of Group
Caucasian	53	50	17
African American	41	39	30
Asian	7	7	17
Hispanic	4	4	15

T A B L E **8-2c**

Monitor results, not how they are obtained. (155)

Category	Number	% of 155	% of Group
Caucasian	98	63	31
African American	36	23	27
Asian	4	3	10
Hispanic	21	11	81

T A B L E **8-2d**

Recommend technology to monitor employees to protect the company's interests and ensure productivity. (231)

Category	Number	% of 231	% of Group
Caucasian	164	71	52
African American	49	21	36
Asian	5	2	12
Hispanic	5	2	19

TABLE **8-2e**

Monitor work to ensure productivity. (160)

Category	Number	% of 160	% of Group
Caucasian	107	67	34
African American	43	27	32
Asian	5	3	12
Hispanic	5	3	19

TABLE **8-2f**

If employees are nonexempt, their hours must be monitored for **Fair Labor Standards Act (FLSA)** purposes. (34)

Category	Number	% of 34	% of Group
Caucasian	13	38	4
African American	12	35	9
Asian	4	12	10
Hispanic	5	15	19

TABLE **8-2g**

Arrange for "face time" in the office for telecommuters. (20)

Category	Number	% of 20	% of Group
Caucasian	13	65	4
African American	3	15	2
Asian	0	0	0
Hispanic	4	20	15

Surprisingly, 88% of the Asian respondents believe that HR should not recommend close monitoring of telecommuters. Research by Akio Kawato suggests that many Asians feel that individual needs or wants should be second to the good of the company, but this cultural belief is beginning to shift with the integration of Western approaches and thought. This may be the case with our second-generation Asian respondents.

A majority of the Hispanic respondents say they would not recommend the use of technology to monitor telecommuters. My Hispanic colleagues attribute this to a cultural inclination toward respect for an individual's output. The work "contract" should be spelled out in terms of measurable outcomes. Close monitoring of work process may seriously jeopardize employee–supervisor relationships.

Eighty-one percent of Hispanic respondents feel it is HR's responsibility to help supervisors set expectations and monitor telecommuters' results. This finding tracks with what my Hispanic colleague advised me—the norm within his culture is to expect those in leadership positions to set parameters and focus on employees' ability to get results.

Almost one-third of the African American respondents believe HR's role is to design an approach to telecommuting that will build trust, compared to 17% of the Caucasian and Asian respondents and 15% of Hispanic respondents. The theme that is most prevalent with the African American respondents in this group is that Human Resources should establish specific guidelines such as when telecommuters can access Web sites for personal use. The guidelines should be addressed during training, after which supervisors need to trust telecommuting employees.

Over one-half of Caucasian respondents believe Human Resources should recommend monitoring technology, compared to 30% of African Americans, 19% of Hispanics, and 12% of Asians. The traditional Protestant work ethic is very much in evidence throughout the comments from the Caucasian respondents, which typically focus on ensuring that the employees do not take advantage of the company and give their full day's work for the day's pay they are receiving.

Fifteen percent of Hispanic respondents suggest that Human Resources design a telecommuting policy that allows for office time for telecommuters, while less than 5% of respondents from each of the other three groups provide this recommendation. There is a strong feeling within this group that it is important to reinforce the impression that the telecommuters are still interested in the work site and are very much a part of the office team. I agree: Constant communication improves the chances that trust will not be lost.

8-3 Breakdown by Gender

Table 8-3 breaks down responses by gender.

TABLE **8-3a**

Do not recommend monitoring technology. (287)

Group	Number	% of 287	% of Group
Male	146	52	88
Female	141	49	40

T A B L E **8-3b**

Work on building trust with telecommuting employees. (105)

Group	Number	% of 105	% of Group
Male	36	34	22
Female	69	66	20

T A B L E **8-3c**

Monitor results, not how they are obtained. (155)

Group	Number	% of 155	% of Group
Male	73	47	47
Female	82	53	23

T A B L E **8-3d**

If managers insist on monitoring the process, recommend against telecommuting at this time. (9)

Group	Number	% of 9	% of Group
Male	2	22	1
Female	7	78	2

T A B L E **8-3e**

Recommend technology to monitor employees to preserve the company's interests and ensure productivity. (231)

Group	Number	% of 231	% of Group
Male	20	9	12
Female	211	91	60

T A B L E **8-3f**

Monitor work to ensure productivity. (160)

Group	Number	% of 160	% of Group
Male	18	11	11
Female	142	89	40

TABLE **8-3g**

If employees are nonexempt, their hours must be monitored for FLSA purposes. (34)

Group	Number	% of 34	% of Group
Male	2	6	1
Female	32	94	9

TABLE **8-3h**

Arrange for "face time" in the office with telecommuters. (20)

Group	Number	% of 20	% of Group
Male	3	15	2
Female	17	85	5

You will note a significant difference between the percentage of men and women that recommend the use of technology to monitor telecommuters. Eighty-eight percent of male respondents believe Human Resources should *not* recommend methods to closely monitor employees, compared to 40% of female respondents. Many of the men commented that they thought surveillance would be too intrusive and those employees have the right to work at home or on site without "big brother" watching every move. The primary reason given by most of the women who recommend against monitoring telecommuters is that close monitoring is demeaning and treats employees like children.

Male respondents are clearly interested in setting expectations and monitoring quantitative results—47% compared to 23% for women. In their book, *Women, Ethics and the Workplace*,[5] Fredrick and Atkinson discuss the different styles of men and women in the workplace. Their research leads them to conclude that men are more typically interested in a rigid hierarchy emphasizing a sense of order and clear expectations, while women are more interested in a fluid structure with an emphasis on relationships. This premise tracks with my findings in the different way that men and women respondents approach this dilemma.

Sixty percent of female respondents believe HR *should* recommend technology to monitor telecommuters, to protect the company's interests. This group believes that productivity must be ensured, even at the

---

5. Fredrick, Candice, and Atkinson, Camille. 1997. *Women, Ethics, and the Workplace*. New York: Praeger Publication, page 48.

expense of employee privacy. Several comments were made in this group that, based on individual experiences, one has to monitor employees closely or they will "goof off." I would like to have a follow-up dialogue at some point with these respondents to explore their management style. Perhaps there is a correlation between their experiences and their approach to leading.

Slightly more women than men recommend that Human Resources should design ways for telecommuters to have "face time" in the office. Female respondents who make this recommendation typically comment that telecommuters should be given opportunities to show they are still a part of the team, and male respondents more often say that "face time" is important for political reasons (to demonstrate that off-site employees still expect to have input into decisions that affect them).

8-4 Breakdown by Number of Years in Human Resources and Age

Table 8-4 breaks down responses by number of years in Human Resources; Table 8-5 shows the breakdown by age.

TABLE **8-4a**

Do not recommend monitoring technology. (287)

Tenure	Number	% of 287	% of Group
0–1	67	23	75
2–3	94	33	92
4–5	29	10	50
6–10	81	28	46
> 10	16	6	17

TABLE **8-4b**

Work on building trust with the telecommuting employees. (105)

Tenure	Number	% of 105	% of Group
0–1	36	34	40
2–3	40	38	39
4–5	7	7	12
6–10	16	15	9
> 10	6	6	6

TABLE **8-4c**

Monitor results, not how they are obtained. (155)

Tenure	Number	% of 155	% of Group
0–1	42	27	47
2–3	47	30	46
4–5	31	20	53
6–10	18	12	10
> 10	17	11	18

TABLE **8-4d**

Recommend technology to monitor employees to protect the company's interests and ensure productivity. (231)

Tenure	Number	% of 231	% of Group
0–1	22	10	25
2–3	8	3	8
4–5	29	13	50
6–10	95	41	54
>10	77	33	83

TABLE **8-4e**

Monitor work to ensure productivity. (160)

Tenure	Number	% of 160	% of Group
0–1	14	9	16
2–3	19	12	19
4–5	28	18	48
6–10	68	43	39
> 10	31	19	33

TABLE **8-4f**

If employees are nonexempt, their hours must be monitored for FLSA purposes. (34)

Tenure	Number	% of 34	% of Group
0–1	13	38	15
2–3	15	44	15
4–5	4	12	7
6–10	2	6	1
>10	0	0	0

TABLE **8-4g**

Arrange for "face time" in the office with telecommuters. (20)

Tenure	Number	% of 20	% of Group
0–1	0	0	0
2–3	4	20	4
4–5	9	45	16
6–10	4	20	2
> 10	3	15	3

TABLE **8-5a**

Do not recommend monitoring technology. (287)

Age	Number	% of 287	% of Group
<30	161	56	84
31–40	110	38	47
41–50	9	3	15
51–60	7	2	21

TABLE **8-5b**

Work on building trust with the telecommuting employees. (105)

Age	Number	% of 105	% of Group
<30	76	72	40
31–40	23	22	10
41–50	2	2	3
51–60	4	4	12

TABLE **8-5c**

Monitor results, not how they are obtained. (155)

Age	Number	% of 155	% of Group
<30	89	57	47
31–40	49	32	21
41–50	12	8	20
51–60	5	3	15

TABLE **8-5d**

Recommend technology to monitor employees to preserve the company's interests and ensure productivity. (231)

Age	Number	% of 231	% of Group
<30	30	13	16
31–40	124	54	53
41–50	50	22	83
51–60	27	12	82

TABLE **8-5e**

Monitor work to ensure productivity. (160)

Age	Number	% of 160	% of Group
<30	33	21	17
31–40	96	60	41
41–50	11	7	18
51–60	20	13	61

TABLE **8-5f**

If employees are nonexempt, their hours must be monitored for FLSA purposes. (34)

Age	Number	% of 34	% of Group
<30	28	82	15
31–40	6	18	2
41–50	0	0	0
51–60	0	0	0

TABLE **8-5g**

Arrange for "face time" in the office with telecommuters. (20)

Age	Number	% of 20	% of Group
<30	4	20	2
31–40	13	65	6
41–50	1	5	2
51–60	2	10	6

Zemke, Raines, and Filipczak, in *Generations at Work,*[6] and Natalie K. Munn, in her Web article entitled "Generation x + Technology = y" (http://members.aol.com, 5/5/99); and the April 1 issue of First Union's *Management Ideas* newsletter (http://www.firstunion.com) suggest that younger workers focus more on results rather than process, so I expected a difference in responses from Generations X and Y and respondents over age 35. In their book, Zemke, Raines, and Filipczak[7] assert that the WWII generation (age 61 plus) believes in personal sacrifice for the company and respects hierarchy and authority. Baby boomers (ages 41–61) believe in working as a team for the good of the company.

Is anyone surprised, then, that 84% of respondents under age 30 believe that Human Resources should not recommend monitoring technology, compared to 21% of respondents between ages 51–60?!

Forty percent of respondents with 1 year or less Human Resource experience suggest that HR's role is to design a telecommuting program that builds trust, compared to only 6% of respondents with over 10 years' experience. These younger respondents have something to teach the rest of us!

The recurring theme among the first group of respondents is that surveillance should not be warranted if the organization hires trustworthy employees and provides resources to complete their work off site. They assert that if expectations are clearly established regarding work outcomes, there should not be a need for any type of monitoring on a day-by-day basis.

The prevalent theme among the second, older, group of respondents is that individuals must give up some privacy for the sake of company productivity. This group asserts that a few individuals, given the latitude to work at home, could bring down the company's productivity levels if they are not monitored (and know they are being monitored).

The 31–40-year-old response group has a close split between those who recommend monitoring and those who do not believe this is required. Forty-one percent believe that productivity could suffer without surveillance, and 47% do not believe Human Resources should have a hand in any type of surveillance. Perhaps some cynicism as to the degree of trust that can be afforded employees comes with years in the field. While 40% of under-30 respondents believe HR can and should design a system that builds trust between managers and telecommuters, only 10% of 31–40-year-old respondents feel this is HR's role.

---

6. Zemke, Raines, and Filipczak, *Generations At Work,* page 84.

7. Ibid., pages 46, 76.

8-5 Breakdown by Organization Type

Table 8-6 breaks down responses by organization type.

TABLE **8-6a**

Do not recommend monitoring technology. (287)

Type	Number	% of 287	% of Group
Mfg	68	24	72
Svc	101	35	51
NFP	32	11	62
PS	86	30	49

TABLE **8-6b**

Work on building trust with telecommuting employees. (105)

Type	Number	% of 105	% of Group
Mfg	3	3	3
Svc	59	56	30
NFP	3	3	6
PS	40	38	23

TABLE **8-6c**

Monitor results, not how they are obtained. (155)

Type	Number	% of 155	% of Group
Mfg	35	23	37
Svc	47	30	24
NFP	20	13	38
PS	53	34	30

TABLE **8-6d**

Recommend technology to monitor employees to protect the company's interests and ensure productivity. (231)

Type	Number	% of 231	% of Group
Mfg	26	11	28
Svc	96	42	49
NFP	20	9	38
PS	89	39	51

TABLE **8-6e**

Monitor work to ensure productivity. (160)

Type	Number	% of 160	% of Group
Mfg	18	11	19
Svc	51	32	26
NFP	7	4	13
PS	84	53	48

TABLE **8-6f**

If the employees are nonexempt, hours must be monitored for FLSA purposes. (34)

Type	Number	% of 34	% of Group
Mfg	8	24	8.5
Svc	19	56	10
NFP	5	15	10
PS	2	6	1

TABLE **8-6g**

Arrange for "face time" in the office with telecommuters. (20)

Type	Number	% of 20	% of Group
Mfg	6	30	6
Svc	6	30	3
NFP	0	0	0
PS	8	40	5

Manufacturing respondents are the least likely to recommend monitoring of telecommuters, followed by nonprofit respondents. Many manufacturing respondents note that few positions in a manufacturing company are amenable to off-site work arrangements—it is hard to "phone in" your work if you are on the assembly line!

Almost one-third of service organization respondents believe HR should find ways to ensure trust between telecommuters and their supervisors, compared to 23% of the public sector group, 6% of the nonprofit group, and 3% of the manufacturing group. Common suggestions from service organization respondents include:

- Hold a training session for both telecommuters and their managers before the program begins.

- Provide coaching for managers on supervision of telecommuters.
- Set clear expectations regarding outcomes and incorporate into the performance instruments.

Just over one-half of the public sector respondents believe HR's role is to protect the organization's interests and recommend monitoring technology. A common theme among this response group is that employees will take advantage of a company given the opportunity. They assert that productivity will most likely suffer unless telecommuters are watched closely. As a former public sector employee myself, I am sorry to discover this reinforcement of the stereotypical nonproductive, unmotivated public employee.

Almost one-half of service organization respondents believe HR should recommend monitoring of telecommuters. Many in this group comment about pilot telecommuting efforts within their own organizations that have been abysmal failures. These unsuccessful efforts have resulted in a lack of confidence that any telecommuting programs can succeed without electronic surveillance.

8-6 Breakdown by Organization Size

Table 8-7 breaks down responses by organization size.

TABLE **8-7a**

Do not recommend monitoring technology. (287)

Category	Number	% of 287	% of Group
1	17	6	59
2	50	17	68
3	108	38	68
4	57	20	42
5	55	19	45

TABLE **8-7b**

Work on building trust with telecommuting employees. (105)

Category	Number	% of 105	% of Group
1	9	9	31
2	31	30	42
3	48	46	30
4	10	10	7
5	7	7	6

TABLE **8-7c**

Monitor results, not how they are obtained. (155)

Category	Number	% of 155	% of Group
1	8	5	28
2	19	12	26
3	60	39	38
4	47	30	35
5	21	14	17

TABLE **8-7d**

Recommend technology to monitor employees to protect company's interests and ensure productivity. (231)

Category	Number	% of 231	% of Group
1	12	5	41
2	23	10	32
3	51	22	32
4	79	34	58
5	66	29	55

TABLE **8-7e**

Monitor work to ensure productivity. (160)

Category	Number	% of 160	% of Group
1	5	3	17
2	16	10	22
3	39	24	25
4	59	37	43
5	41	26	34

TABLE **8-7f**

If employees are nonexempt, hours must be monitored for FLSA purposes. (34)

Category	Number	% of 34	% of Group
1	4	12	14
2	4	12	5
3	8	24	5
4	11	32	8
5	7	21	6

TABLE **8-7g**

Arrange for "face time" in the office for telecommuters. (20)

Category	Number	% of 20	% of Group
1	3	15	10
2	4	20	5
3	5	25	3
4	8	40	6
5	0	0	0

Because larger organizations may experience difficulty managing an on-site workforce, let alone telecommuters, I expected that respondents from large companies would recommend employee monitoring more than those from smaller companies. I also thought that smaller company representatives would suggest that results are the appropriate yardstick to measure success, not process. The results are mixed and do not necessarily support my expectations. I believe that widespread buy-in for telecommuting just does not exist across organizations in the United States—at least, not yet.

Respondents from organizations that have 101–1,000 employees are least likely to support using technology to monitor telecommuters. Fifty-nine percent of respondents from the smallest organizations believe monitoring would tear down trust and be de-motivating for employees. As company size increases, the belief that building trust is HR's role decreases. Some respondents from the 5,000+ employee companies lament that it would be nice to trust employees across the board, but hedging the bet with monitoring is probably necessary.

Thirty-eight percent of 501–1,000 employee company representatives believe that results, rather than how and when during the day results are obtained, should be monitored, compared to 28% of 0–100 employee company representatives. Typical responses from the former group are, "It's too time consuming to review factors like log-on and log-out times," and "Who cares how and when during the work day results are achieved."

Only a small percentage (20 people) in the total population suggest Human Resources should take responsibility for creating opportunities for telecommuter "face time" in the office. Ten percent of respondents from the smallest company category believe this is HR's job, compared to zero respondents in the 5,001–10,000 employee category. Many respondents from larger companies comment that HR does not have time to supervise the overall telecommuting process.

Chapter Summary

This dilemma forces a balancing act between employee privacy and company productivity. The Human Resource practitioner is asked to determine which is most important, given the growth of technology and its concomitant surveillance options. In their book on the virtual workplace, Crandall and Wallace acknowledge that ". . . building trust between managers and employees is one of the biggest challenges in implementing a telecommuting program."[8]

Just over one-half of our response set believes HR should not recommend technology to monitor telecommuters and should instead design ways to build trust between supervisors and direct reports who work off site. This group believes that the role of Human Resources is to manage the process by monitoring results rather than monitoring how employees obtain results. I absolutely agree with this approach, as I strongly believe that a cornerstone of an ethical organization is trust between management and employees.

Forty-five percent of our response set, however, does believe that HR should recommend monitoring technology. In the demographic breakdowns, we find that Caucasians, women, and 51- to 60-year-olds are the most likely groups to promote monitoring via technology. Manufacturing company respondents are the practitioners who are least likely to recommend the use of monitoring technology.

Discussion Questions

1. Is it a myth that employees who are out of the supervisor's sight will not be as productive as on-site workers?
2. Which role do you think Human Resources should adopt in this scenario—"big brother" or advocate for employee privacy?
3. What dilemmas have you observed in organizations stemming from technological advancements?

---

8. Crandall and Wallace, *Work and Rewards in the Virtual Workplace*, page 51.

Chapter 9

Ethical Dilemma #7: Can Human Resources Allow Self-Directed Teams to *Really* be Self-Directed?

Key Term

Self-directed teams

Outline

9-1 Breakdown by Total
9-2 Breakdown by Gender
9-3 Breakdown by Race and Ethnicity
9-4 Breakdown by Number of Years in Human Resources and Age
9-5 Breakdown by Organization Type
9-6 Breakdown by Organization Size
Chapter Summary
Discussion Questions

*Your organization has formed **self-directed** work teams that have a great deal of input into hiring and termination decisions, as well as rotation of team members across the organization. You have heard rumors in the lunchroom that two of the teams are experiencing internal conflict and they are making recommendations based on personal likes and dislikes as opposed to peoples' skills. Should Human Resources intervene?*

Many U.S. organizations have one form or another of cross-functional work teams. In some cases, team members assist in the employee selection process and provide input to Human Resources about moving individuals off the team. While this can promote accountability for team success (or failure), line managers and Human Resources must walk a fine line between coaching team members and directing their decisions. In an article on self-directed work teams (www.worldtrans.org), Frank Heckman promotes the use of self-directed teams to enhance productivity, improve employees' understanding of their jobs, and elevate employees' pride in their work.

9-1 Breakdown by Total

Table 9-1 breaks down responses by total.

TABLE **9-1**   Breakdown by Total

HR should not intervene	25%
HR should intervene	75%
HR should meet with and counsel team	64%
HR should coach on an ongoing basis	43%

Three-fourths of the respondents believe it is HR's role to intervene, and diverse views are offered about the form this intervention should take. Several reasons are offered by respondents as to why HR cannot simply stand by and hope team members decide to make the right choices.

Reasons offered most often are:

- This situation is a learning opportunity that should not be ignored.
- Disparate impact or disparate treatment may be occurring.

The intervention recommended by most of the 386 respondents who think HR should intervene is to meet with each team as a whole, verify their current selection criteria, and counsel them on ways to focus on specific skills and competencies when making selection recommendations. These respondents believe that HR's role in this meeting is (1) to serve as a coach to ensure that team members make decisions in the first instance and (2) to make decisions that are good for the teams and also keep the organization out of legal trouble.

The intervention suggested by 43% of the respondents is to become a coach on an ongoing basis or assign another person with appropriate skills to this role. This action is viewed as part of HR's role as an internal consultant, they believe, to proactively offer guidance when a need surfaces. Interestingly, these respondents assume that the rumor is true and that the teams require guidance.

One-fourth of the respondents do *not* believe HR should intervene in the teams' decision-making process in any way. This group believes Human Resources would be perceived as meddling, and this may damage the teams' morale. Within this response group, 60 respondents suggest that HR should wait until help is requested before taking any action.

9-2 Breakdown by Gender

As with the previous six dilemmas, interesting differences emerge between genders (Table 9-2).

TABLE **9-2a**

Human Resources should intervene. (386)

Group	Number	% of 386	% of Group
Male	116	30	70
Female	270	70	77

Method of Intervention:

T A B L E **9-2b**

Provide teams with a criteria checklist for all interviews. (47)

Group	Number	% of 47	% of Group
Male	41	87	25
Female	6	13	2

T A B L E **9-2c**

Develop a policy that states that either HR or a manager always retains ultimate oversight of teams. (25)

Group	Number	% of 25	% of Group
Male	18	72	11
Female	7	28	2

T A B L E **9-2d**

Notify managers who have team oversight and counsel them about how to handle the situation. (50)

Group	Number	% of 50	% of Group
Male	13	26	8
Female	37	74	10.5

T A B L E **9-2e**

Offer team-building training. (53)

Group	Number	% of 53	% of Group
Male	13	24.5	8
Female	40	75.5	11

T A B L E **9-2f**

Sit in on meetings or serve as a consultant. (59)

Group	Number	% of 59	% of Group
Male	23	39	14
Female	36	61	10

TABLE **9-2g**

Provide a training session for teams on selecting and hiring. (116)

Group	Number	% of 116	% of Group
Male	54	47	47
Female	62	53	18

TABLE **9-2h**

Verify that the rumors are true, then counsel the team members on how to focus on specific skills as criteria for hiring. (331)

Group	Number	% of 331	% of Group
Male	136	41	82
Female	195	59	55

TABLE **9-2i**

Become a coach on an ongoing basis or assign one. (166)

Group	Number	% of 166	% of Group
Male	69	42	42
Female	97	58	28

TABLE **9-2j**

Human Resources should not intervene—it might destroy team morale and be viewed as meddling. (132)

Group	Number	% of 132	% of Group
Male	50	28	30
Female	82	72	23

The response rate in favor of Human Resources intervening is about the same for men and women. The significant differences occur in the recommended types of intervention.

One-fourth of the male respondents suggest providing teams with a criteria checklist for use in the interview process, compared to 2% of female respondents. The reasoning the men offered most is that HR should be helpful but should not insert itself into the team activities. The reasoning offered by the (small) group of women in this category is that team members do not frequently conduct recruiting activities, so they may need a reminder of hiring criteria.

Two-and-a-half times as many men as women believe Human Resources should develop a policy that states either Human Resources or a line manager will retain ultimate oversight of teams. The male respondents are concerned that team members will only consider personalities when making new hire recommendations, and they cannot be entrusted with staffing decisions. Female respondents' comments focus more on allowing team members to spend their time achieving the team's work instead of staffing the team.

Almost half of the men suggest providing a training session on selection and hiring methods, compared to 53% of women. Even though the response rate is close on this suggestion, the objective behind the recommendation differs between men and women. Men more often suggest training to minimize the danger of the teams violating Title VII requirements. Women more often recommend training to build team members' confidence in their abilities to help select coworkers.

Female respondents' suggestions are more oriented toward coaching managers to handle the situation or offering team-building training. The women are more likely to focus on a subtle, behind-the-scenes role for Human Resources, while male respondents want to take charge of the process. This finding supports the assertion by Gary Vikesland in his article, "Supervising Men" (www.employer-employee.com) that women tend to find value in equality when they communicate with coworkers and direct reports, while men tend more toward emphasizing the chain of command and establishing a "pecking order."

9-3 Breakdown by Race and Ethnicity

Table 9-3 breaks down responses by race and ethnicity.

TABLE **9-3a**

Human Resources should intervene. (386—75% of 518!)

Category	Number	% of 386	% of Group
Caucasian	209	54	66
African American	127	33	94
Asian	32	8	78
Hispanic	18	5	69

TABLE **9-3b**

Provide teams with a criteria checklist for all interviews. (47)

Category	Number	% of 47	% of Group
Caucasian	26	55	8
African American	15	32	11
Asian	2	4	5
Hispanic	4	8	15

TABLE **9-3c**

Develop a policy that states that either HR or a manager always retains ultimate oversight of teams (25).

Category	Number	% of 25	% of Group
Caucasian	16	64	5
African American	5	20	4
Asian	3	12	7
Hispanic	1	4	4

TABLE **9-3d**

Notify managers who have team oversight and counsel them about how to handle the situation. (50)

Category	Number	% of 50	% of Group
Caucasian	17	34	5
African American	28	56	21
Asian	0	0	0
Hispanic	5	10	19

TABLE **9-3e**

Offer team-building training. (53)

Category	Number	% of 53	% of Group
Caucasian	21	40	7
African American	16	30	12
Asian	9	17	22
Hispanic	7	13	27

TABLE **9-3f**

Sit in on team meetings or serve as a team consultant. (59)

Category	Number	% of 59	% of Group
Caucasian	23	39	7
African American	18	31	13
Asian	11	19	27
Hispanic	7	12	27

TABLE **9-3g**

Provide a training session for teams on selection and hiring. (116)

Category	Number	% of 116	% of Group
Caucasian	90	78	28
African American	19	16	14
Asian	3	3	7
Hispanic	4	3	15

TABLE **9-3h**

Verify that the rumors are true, then counsel the team members on how to focus on specific skills as criteria for hiring. (331)

Category	Number	% of 331	% of Group
Caucasian	203	61	64
African American	111	34	82
Asian	11	3	27
Hispanic	6	2	23

TABLE **9-3i**

Become a coach on an ongoing basis or assign one. (166)

Category	Number	% of 166	% of Group
Caucasian	63	38	20
African American	67	40	50
Asian	19	11	46
Hispanic	17	10	65

T A B L E **9-3j**

Human Resources should not intervene—it might destroy team morale and be viewed as meddling. (132)

Category	Number	% of 132	% of Group
Caucasian	107	81	34
African American	8	6	6
Asian	9	7	22
Hispanic	8	6	31

A majority of all four groups believes it is HR's role to intervene; however, African Americans have the largest group percentage (94%) that makes this recommendation.

Reasons most often cited for intervention by African American respondents are:

- HR must intercede to protect the organization.
- If a few immature employees are allowed to make poor decisions, the teams will not be effective.

Most African American respondents favor counseling team members on how to objectively focus on applicants' skills and competencies during the selection process. Several respondents in this group say that they believe Human Resources needs to intervene any time that individuals who are acting in an unacceptable manner damage the integrity of the entire organization.

The recommendation made most often by Hispanic respondents is for Human Resources to provide a criteria checklist for the teams to use during the interview process, in addition to offering team-building training or coaching. Reasons most often provided by this response group in support of this approach are: It is necessary to set clear expectations for decisions so team members are not tempted to be persuaded by personality preferences; and team members need firm, but polite, direction to keep them from making errors in judgment. This response tracks with Hispanics' approach to our other dilemmas—provide polite, but firm, expectations and allow people to do their jobs.

As with their responses to previous scenarios, Asian respondents most often gravitate toward interventions for the protection of the organization, such as Human Resources or a line manager retaining ultimate oversight of team decisions or maintaining a presence in team meetings. The response group's primary reason for this recommendation is that the teams' actions could result in legal problems for the company.

Almost one-third of Hispanic and just over one-third of Caucasian respondents believe Human Resources should *not* intervene because this could be perceived as meddling. These two groups feel strongly that Human Resources should not react to rumors but should instead let team members come forward when problems arise.

9-4 Breakdown by Number of Years in Human Resources and Age

Table 9-4 breaks down responses by the number of years in Human Resources; Table 9-5 shows the breakdown by age.

TABLE **9-4a**

Human Resources should intervene. (386)

Tenure	Number	% of 386	% of Group
0–1	54	14	61
2–3	75	19	74
4–5	43	11	74
6–10	138	36	78
> 10	76	20	82

TABLE **9-4b**

Provide teams with a criteria checklist for all interviews. (47)

Tenure	Number	% of 47	% of Group
0–1	27	57	30
2–3	8	17	8
4–5	6	13	10
6–10	4	9	2
> 10	2	4	2

TABLE **9-4c**

Develop a policy that states that either HR or a manager always retains ultimate oversight of teams. (25)

Tenure	Number	% of 25	% of Group
0–1	7	28	8
2–3	6	24	6
4–5	5	20	9
6–10	3	12	2
> 10	4	16	4

T A B L E **9-4d**

Notify managers who have team oversight and counsel them about how to handle the situation. (50)

Tenure	Number	% of 50	% of Group
0–1	1	2	1
2–3	3	6	3
4–5	9	18	15.5
6–10	16	32	9
> 10	21	42	23

T A B L E **9-4e**

Offer team-building training. (53)

Tenure	Number	% of 53	% of Group
0–1	5	9	6
2–3	0	0	0
4–5	9	17	15.5
6–10	26	49	15
> 10	13	25	14

T A B L E **9-4f**

Sit in on meetings and/or serve as a consultant. (59)

Tenure	Number	% of 59	% of Group
0–1	4	7	4
2–3	7	12	7
4–5	7	12	12
6–10	23	39	13
> 10	18	31	19

T A B L E **9-4g**

Provide a training session for teams on selecting and hiring. (116)

Tenure	Number	% of 116	% of Group
0–1	8	7	9
2–3	5	4	5
4–5	24	21	41
6–10	36	31	20
> 10	43	37	46

TABLE **9-4h**

Verify that the rumors are true, then counsel the team members on how to focus on specific skills as criteria for hiring. (331)

Tenure	Number	% of 331	% of Group
0–1	39	12	44
2–3	87	26	85
4–5	46	14	79
6–10	125	38	71
> 10	34	10	37

TABLE **9-4i**

Become a coach on an ongoing basis or assign one. (166)

Tenure	Number	% of 166	% of Group
0–1	45	27	51
2–3	12	7	12
4–5	10	6	17
6–10	58	35	33
> 10	41	25	44

TABLE **9-4j**

Human Resources should not intervene—it might destroy team morale and be viewed as meddling. (132)

Tenure	Number	% of 132	% of Group
0–1	35	27	39
2–3	27	20	26
4–5	15	11	26
6–10	38	29	22
> 10	17	13	18

TABLE **9-5a**

Human Resources should intervene. (386)

Age	Number	% of 386	% of Group
<30	129	33	67.5
31–40	181	47	77
41–50	48	12	80
51–60	28	7	85

TABLE **9-5b**

Provide teams with a criteria checklist for all interviews. (47)

Age	Number	% of 47	% of Group
<30	35	74	18
31–40	10	21	4
41–50	2	4	3
51–60	0	0	0

TABLE **9-5c**

Develop a policy that states that either HR or a manager always retains ultimate oversight of teams. (25)

Age	Number	% of 25	% of Group
<30	13	52	7
31–40	8	32	3
41–50	1	4	2
51–60	3	12	9

TABLE **9-5d**

Notify managers who have team oversight and counsel them about how to handle the situation. (50)

Age	Number	% of 50	% of Group
<30	4	8	2
31–40	25	50	11
41–50	9	18	15
51–60	12	24	36

TABLE **9-5e**

Offer team-building training. (53)

Age	Number	% of 53	% of Group
<30	5	9	3
31–40	35	66	15
41–50	10	19	17
51–60	3	6	9

TABLE **9-5f**

Sit in on meetings and/or serve as a consultant. (59)

Age	Number	% of 59	% of Group
<30	11	19	6
31–40	30	51	13
41–50	6	10	10
51–60	12	20	36

TABLE **9-5g**

Provide a training session for teams on selecting and hiring. (116)

Age	Number	% of 116	% of Group
<30	13	11	7
31–40	60	52	26
41–50	22	19	37
51–60	21	18	64

TABLE **9-5h**

Verify that the rumors are true, then counsel the team members on how to focus on specific skills as criteria for hiring. (331)

Age	Number	% of 331	% of Group
<30	126	38	66
31–40	171	52	73
41–50	15	5	25
51–60	19	6	58

TABLE **9-5i**

Become a coach on an ongoing basis or assign one. (166)

Age	Number	% of 166	% of Group
<30	57	34	30
31–40	68	41	29
41–50	38	23	63
51–60	3	2	9

TABLE **9-5j**

Human Resources should not intervene—it might destroy team morale and be viewed as meddling. (132)

Age	Number	% of 132	% of Group
<30	60	45	31
31–40	53	40	23
41–50	11	8	18
51–60	6	5	18

A majority of each age and experience group believes it is HR's role to intervene. However, the group that is strongest in this belief is the 51- to 60-year-old age group (85%). As with other demographic groups, the type and extent of the intervention suggested by different age groups vary.

The respondents under age 30 who believe HR should intervene most often recommend providing teams with a criteria checklist to use during interviews. The primary impetus behind this suggestion is offering specific guidelines around what is expected. In my interviews with Generation Y and Generation X workers across the country, the plaintive plea of many was this: Just tell me what you expect, then get out of my way.

Over one-third of the respondents with 1 year or less of Human Resources experience do not believe HR should intervene, and 18% of this group does not recommend taking action until HR's assistance is requested by the teams.

Almost one-half of the most experienced group suggests Human Resources should provide team training on selecting and hiring methods. Many in this response set also suggest interventions such as counseling managers with team oversight responsibility and sitting in on meetings to offer guidance. The comments from this older, more seasoned group were almost parental in tone. They seem to say, "We've been there, done that—let us help you." In my interviews during 2000 with 500 Baby Boomers, one management approach surfaced repeatedly as the preferred style: participative management. This is how Boomers told me they want to work and the way they assume coworkers and direct reports prefer to work.

9-5 Breakdown by Organization Type

Table 9-6 breaks down responses by organization type.

T A B L E **9-6a**

Human Resources should intervene. (386)

Type	Number	% of 386	% of Group
Mfg	21	5	22
Svc	177	46	90
NFP	43	11	83
PS	145	38	83

T A B L E **9-6b**

Provide teams with a criteria checklist for all interviews. (47)

Type	Number	% of 47	% of Group
Mfg	0	0	0
Svc	29	62	15
NFP	0	0	0
PS	18	38	10

T A B L E **9-6c**

Develop a policy that states that either HR or a manager always retains ultimate oversight of teams. (25)

Type	Number	% of 25	% of Group
Mfg	13	52	14
Svc	2	8	1
NFP	2	8	4
PS	8	32	5

T A B L E **9-6d**

Notify managers who have team oversight and counsel them about how to handle the situation. (50)

Type	Number	% of 50	% of Group
Mfg	1	2	1
Svc	13	26	7
NFP	8	16	15
PS	28	56	16

T A B L E **9-6e**

Offer team-building training. (53)

Type	Number	% of 53	% of Group
Mfg	14	26	15
Svc	26	49	13
NFP	3	6	6
PS	10	19	6

T A B L E **9-6f**

Sit in on meetings and/or serve as a consultant. (59)

Type	Number	% of 59	% of Group
Mfg	12	20	13
Svc	31	53	16
NFP	10	17	19
PS	5	8	3

T A B L E **9-6g**

Provide a training session for teams on selecting and hiring. (116)

Type	Number	% of 116	% of Group
Mfg	15	13	16
Svc	48	41	24
NFP	14	12	27
PS	39	34	22

T A B L E **9-6h**

Verify that the rumors are true, then counsel the team members on how to focus on specific skills as criteria for hiring. (331)

Type	Number	% of 331	% of Group
Mfg	21	6	22
Svc	165	50	84
NFP	40	12	77
PS	105	32	60

TABLE **9-6i**

Become a coach on an ongoing basis or assign one. (166)

Type	Number	% of 166	% of Group
Mfg	0	0	0
Svc	78	47	40
NFP	5	3	10
PS	83	50	47

TABLE **9-6j**

HR should not intervene—it might destroy team morale and be viewed as meddling. (132)

Type	Number	% of 132	% of Group
Mfg	73	55	78
Svc	20	15	10
NFP	9	7	17
PS	30	23	17

A majority of respondents in each organization type represented suggests intervention by Human Resources, *except* those from manufacturing. Respondents from manufacturing companies most often cited these reasons for not intervening:

- Rumors fly in organizations, and HR cannot spend time chasing rumors
- HR will come to be viewed as "the police" if it is always chiding people

Most of the service organization respondents believe Human Resources should proactively intercede in the team process. Typical of the points made by respondents in support of this approach are: a few people can damage the entire company's reputation if they are not stopped; and HR needs to be aware of the truth or falsehood of rumors of this nature.

The intervention selected most often across all respondents is counseling for team members to help them focus on specific skills and competencies in the hiring process. Service company respondents have the highest group percentage with this suggestion, and the reason most often provided is protection of the company's image as a fair employer. A high percentage of service company respondents caution that an organization's reputation can be tarnished within the community quickly if it allows individuals to arbitrarily make personnel decisions. About one-half of the respondents in this response set also recommend that Human Resources become a coach on an ongoing basis (or assign one).

9-6 Breakdown by Organization Size

Table 9-7 breaks down responses by organization size.

TABLE **9-7a**

Human Resources should intervene. (386)

Category	Number	% of 386	% of Group
1	22	6	76
2	61	16	84
3	140	36	88
4	115	30	85
5	48	12	40

TABLE **9-7b**

Provide teams with a criteria checklist for all interviews. (47)

Category	Number	% of 47	% of Group
1	2	4	7
2	4	9	5
3	9	19	6
4	14	30	10
5	18	38	15

TABLE **9-7c**

Develop a policy that states that either HR or a manager always retains ultimate oversight of teams. (25)

Category	Number	% of 25	% of Group
1	9	36	31
2	6	24	8
3	3	12	2
4	4	16	3
5	3	12	2

TABLE **9-7d**

Notify managers who have team oversight and counsel them on how to handle the situation. (50)

Category	Number	% of 50	% of Group
1	1	2	3
2	4	8	5
3	8	16	5
4	16	32	12
5	21	42	17

TABLE **9-7e**

Offer team-building training. (53)

Category	Number	% of 53	% of Group
1	2	4	7
2	6	11	8
3	12	23	8
4	14	26	10
5	19	36	16

TABLE **9-7f**

Sit in on meetings and/or serve as a consultant. (59)

Category	Number	% of 59	% of Group
1	4	7	14
2	0	0	0
3	16	27	10
4	15	25	11
5	24	41	20

TABLE **9-7g**

Verify that the rumors are true, then counsel team members on how to focus on specific skills as the criteria for hiring. (331)

Category	Number	% of 331	% of Group
1	24	7	83
2	59	18	81
3	105	32	66
4	98	30	72
5	45	14	37

TABLE **9-7h**

Become a coach on an ongoing basis or assign one. (166)

Category	Number	% of 166	% of Group
1	16	10	55
2	18	11	25
3	31	19	19
4	43	26	32
5	58	35	48

TABLE **9-7i**

HR should not intervene—it might destroy team morale and be seen as meddling. (132)

Category	Number	% of 132	% of Group
1	7	5	24
2	12	9	16
3	19	14	12
4	21	16	15
5	73	55	60

I thought that respondents from the largest organizations would not be as likely to suggest intervention by Human Resources as small company representatives. The demands on HR are many in large companies, and time is limited. My expectation was met: Only 40% of respondents from the largest category, as compared to 76% from the smallest category, believe HR should get involved at this point.

The major theme from comments offered by practitioners from the largest companies is one of priorities. As with the scenario depicted in Chapter 5, Human Resources is hearing secondhand rumors. In this case, the rumor is about team staffing issues. Thirty of the 48 respondents from the category 5 organizations believe that HR's time should be directed toward known problems rather than verifying rumors. However, 15 of the 22 respondents from category 1 organizations suggest that HR should proactively follow up on rumors and either take steps to dispel false rumors or proactively take action when rumors have some validity.

Fifteen percent of the respondents from category 5 organizations suggest that HR's responsibility is to provide a criteria checklist for team use during the interview process. Another 17% from this category recommend notifying managers that have team oversight about the rumor and coaching them about the most appropriate way to follow up with the situation. This group believes only a minimal role for HR is appropriate, opting instead for a coaching role.

Almost one-third of category 1 respondents believes Human Resources should develop a policy that spells out who has ultimate oversight of teams. This group believes it is necessary to retain management oversight for either Human Resources or a line manager. Eighty-three percent of category 1 respondents believe HR's role is to either become a coach on an ongoing basis or assign one to the "problem" teams. Less than 50% of the category 5 practitioners make the same suggestion.

Comments from smaller organization representatives revolve around HR's role in safeguarding company image within the community and ensuring future recruiting potential. Comments from larger organization representatives focus on ensuring that managers across the organization develop coaching and mentoring capabilities so that HR is not the sole resource when team members require assistance.

Chapter Summary

The scenario in this chapter forces survey respondents to balance the need for management control with team autonomy. On the one hand, the organization must prevent discriminatory hiring and promotion activities. On the other hand, self-directed teams are by definition autonomous, decision-making units.

I find it interesting that in this scenario, the majority of our respondents recommend an approach that seemingly leans on the side of the organization rather than an individual or group of individuals. In the first six scenarios, most survey responses support Human Resources more strongly as an employee advocate rather than a company "by the book" representative. I do not find this contradictory, though, because the result of intervention is to ensure that one group of employees—team members who honestly try to be productive—is treated fairly.

Seventy-five percent of the entire response set believes that Human Resources must intervene in the team process to protect the company's interests. The intervention favored by over 80% of respondents is to verify whether the rumor is accurate and then hold counseling sessions with the teams to provide pointers on objective hiring criteria.

Differences across demographic groups are apparent with regard to the degree of direction that Human Resources should provide. For instance, men more often recommend team training to minimize the danger of Title VII violations while women suggest training to build employees' confidence in their hiring capabilities. Both perspectives are entirely valid.

A higher percentage of African Americans than the other three ethnic groups believes Human Resources needs to intervene, and 51- to 60-year-olds comprise the age group that is most strongly in favor of intervention. As I watched *Survivor in Africa*, the popular 2001 TV phenomenon, I predicted early on that a line would be drawn between the Generation X survivors and the older tribe members. The main complaint of the younger members was that older members hovered too much. The retort of the older members? The younger folks would not have done anything if they had not hovered! In this scenario, as well as previous ones, I could not help but notice a similar "line in the sand" between generations.

A majority of each organization type represented suggests intervention by Human Resources, except manufacturing respondents. With regard to differences across organizations of various sizes, smaller company respondents are more in favor of intervention than those from larger companies.

Discussion Questions

1. What will be the effect on the self-directed teams if Human Resources assumes the rumors are true and acts on that assumption?
2. In your opinion, will team autonomy be seriously jeopardized if a Human Resources representative becomes a part of team meetings?
3. How can Human Resources demonstrate that it trusts team members while still protecting the company from legal liability?

The Human Resource Professional's Role in Building an Ethical Organization

Outline

10-1 Core Values
10-2 Mutual Trust and Respect
10-3 Clear Expectations
10-4 Open Communications
10-5 Ongoing Education
10-6 So What Does This Mean to Me—The Human Resource Practitioner?

In Chapter 1, I offered my belief that the two cornerstones of an ethical organization are mutual trust and respect—between individuals and across groups within the organization. This state will not occur spontaneously or maintain itself without ongoing, intentional efforts.

Chapter 10 discusses my framework for creating and maintaining an ethical organization. Let's discuss each component, beginning with core values.

10-1 Core Values

Martin Luther King, Jr. once said:

"If you want to move people, it has to be toward a vision that's positive for them, that taps important values, that gets them something they desire, and it has to be presented in a compelling way that they feel inspired to follow." (Foreword to 2000 National Business Ethics Survey, www.ethics.org).[1]

An organization's core values are manifested by its culture; that is, in the basic ways that business is handled, how decisions are made, how rewards are distributed, and how communication flows (Figure 10-1). Employees learn these ways of doing business through observing coworkers and leaders. If no expectations are established, effectively communicated, and modeled, employees will "make it up as they go along" when faced with ethical dilemmas.

Amy Zipkin, in an October 18, 2000 article for *The New York Times*,[2] says:

"...a growing number of big companies are enacting strict ethical guidelines and backing them up with internal mechanisms to enforce them. While some consider the changes little more than window dressing, there is no doubt that change is afoot."

---

1. King, Martin Luther, Jr. Foreword to National Business Ethics Seminar, 2000.

2. Zipkin, Amy. 2000, October 18. *The New York Times*.

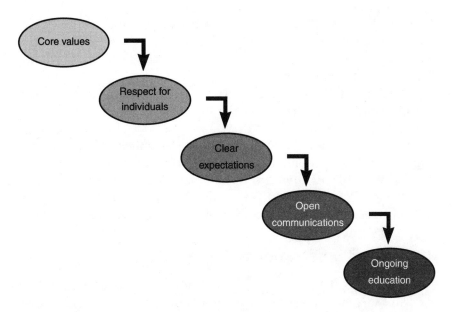

Figure 10-1   Ethical framework suggested by the author.

I have personally observed that many companies today have, or are developing, a Code of Ethics. Several organizations have shared with me their Code of Ethics or Values Statements. Appendix B contains samples that I believe to be eloquent in their simplicity. The components these documents have in common are:

- Mission and Vision
- Specific examples of expected behaviors
- Expectations of leadership
- Contact person(s) for questions and guidance

10-2 Mutual Trust and Respect

How many times have you heard this phrase: "You have to earn respect." My view is somewhat different. I will afford individuals I meet respect as a human being automatically. People may engage in behaviors that result in my loss of respect as time goes by; however, initially my respect for them is a given. Supervisors and managers in organizations are often afforded a level of respect from employees because of their leadership position. I believe that Human Resource professionals are in leadership roles by virtue of visibility and influence, if not always in terms of title. Employees look to the organization's leadership as role models to guide their own behavior. This is especially true when organizations are weathering difficult times, such as mergers or acquisitions, according to the 2000 National Business Ethics Survey, which was conducted by The Ethics Resource Center (www.ethics.org).

The National Business Ethics Survey also finds a correlation between organizational commitment and the modeling of ethical behavior by those in leadership positions. In short, a written Code of Ethics cannot be institutionalized unless organization leaders show their respect for individuals and the organization by engaging in legal *and* moral behaviors.

I have heard this comment many times: "I like her, but I wouldn't trust her to (fill in the blank)." In an ethical organization, employees can depend on each other to put action behind their words.

10-3 Clear Expectations

Putting a Code of Ethics in place and ensuring that leaders are clearly modeling an ethical organization are important steps toward creating an ethical workplace. Each employee must then understand his or her role in carrying out the organization's values—that is, expectations around standards of behavior in everyday situations must be established.

In our scenario about telecommuters, for example, employees who work at home should have clear expectations set by their supervisors around output, communication with on-site employees, and interaction with external customers. Concrete goals and measures must be set *before* the telecommuting program commences. If "gray areas" emerge as the positions are evolving, telecommuters need to know their degree of autonomy and when it is necessary to call on their supervisor. Establishing these guidelines at the onset can, in turn, build mutual trust.

Organizations have numerous opportunities to establish and communicate expectations regarding employees' ethical behavior. One opportunity occurs during the recruiting process. Place your organization's Code of Ethics on your Web site, alongside information about the organization's Mission and Vision. Include the Code of Ethics in your employee handbook and review it as part of the new employee orientation. When inappropriate behavior occurs, do not ignore it—that implies you condone the employee's actions. Meet with the employee and have a frank discussion about the company's values, specifically how the employee has breached those values, and expected future behavior.

The National Business Ethics Survey finds that employees have high expectations for their organizations. Ninety percent say they expect their organizations to do "what is right, not just what is profitable."

10-4 Open Communications

After expectations are initially established, ongoing and open communication systems must be in place to ensure a forum for discussion exists regarding ethical issues. For example, if an employee's immediate supervisor engages in unethical behavior, does the employee have a course of action in terms of communicating this breach of ethics? Employees should not be afraid of reprisals if they report unethical practices, so a confidential system to report problems should be established.

Informal meetings and accessibility are two ways that supervisors can keep the channels of communication flowing. In the 1980s Tom Peters popularized the phrase "management by walking around." The Human Resources staff can increase its visibility by delivering information, training, or messages personally from time to time so that employees have an opportunity to see HR in roles other than the "police." An increased employee comfort level with Human Resources will result in more open discussion about questions, issues, or concerns. As a Human Resource professional, you have an opportunity through the stories you tell and the events that you comment about to illustrate what matters to you and what you consider acceptable behavior.

Human Resource professionals have a unique opportunity to influence the trust level within their organization. If HR's communications—about downsizing, for instance—are truthful, this helps to build trust.

10-5 Ongoing Education

Human Resource practitioners will constantly face new and challenging ethical dilemmas in the 21st century. Ongoing education for management and employees will keep ethical standards and core values in the forefront of workplace life.

Results of the 2000 National Business Ethics Survey are markedly different than 1994 results. The 2000 survey finds that significantly more companies have written ethics standards and conduct ongoing ethics training. The 2000 survey also finds that in 1999, one in three employees observed behaviors that violated either the Code of Ethics or the law. Almost half of these employees did not report this misconduct! I view this as a clear indicator that Human Resources cannot become complacent just because expectations have been committed to writing.

The October 18, 2000 *The New York Times*[3] article by Amy Zipkin relates how leaders in companies today are educating employees about

---

3. Ibid.

core values. Two examples noted are Lockheed Martin and McMurray Publishing Company. Lockheed Martin has created a newspaper called *Ethics Daily* that prints articles about actual ethical dilemmas faced by its employees. The newsletter invites employee input about appropriate ways to handle the dilemmas, and HR uses the scenarios in ongoing training activities. McMurray Publishing Company requires that all employees attend a meeting every other Monday during which ethical dilemmas—and how to resolve them—are discussed.

10-6 So What Does This Mean to Me— The Human Resource Practitioner?

In 1991, the Society for Human Resource Management (www.shrm.org) partnered with Commerce Clearing House to conduct a survey of U.S. Human Resource professionals. Forty-two percent of respondents in a sample size of 1073 reported that ethics training was initiated by Human Resources. If this survey were to be conducted tomorrow, I hope a much higher percentage of Human Resource practitioners report this activity as a significant aspect of their role.

Each individual's response to everyday situations contributes to an organization's ethical viability. As an individual, you have to sleep with decisions you make each day. As a Human Resource professional, you can ask yourself these crucial questions to guide decisions you must make:

1. What are the facts?
2. What else do I need to know?
3. Who are the people affected (stakeholders)?
4. What are the values of the organization?
5. What are *my* values?

In *The Ethics of Excellence*, Price Pritchett says: "Part of your job is to help set, promote, and enforce the ethics of excellence. Whether you like it or not, you will be one of the architects of the corporate conscience." I agree, and I also understand that this is an awesome responsibility. Human Resources, as a profession, is facing a workplace in which:

- Technology is moving at warp speed.
- Organizations have fewer levels of management and are pushing decision making down to line employees.
- Virtual offices are more commonplace.
- A stressful, fast-paced environment leaves individuals feeling isolated and alone.

- Complex issues, such as using the results of genetic testing to make employment decisions, are on the horizon.

This is the backdrop against which we will do our work. We can succeed if we travel the next decade equipped with a strong sense of ethics that is clear to ourselves and to those with whom we come in contact.

My intention with this book is to provide readers with a sense of how others in the Human Resource Management profession feel about handling dilemmas that are prevalent in today's world. My hope is that you can use this information, along with the guidelines I have offered, to help you establish your own ethical framework. Then you will know with certainty what type of organization is for you (and if you are fortunate, you are already working in that organization).

I have a great deal of faith in the Human Resources profession. We *can* help build ethical organizations because we must.

Ethical Dilemmas of 21st Century Human Resource Professionals— Survey of Current Practices

Part I—Demographic Information

Industry: ____ Manufacturing   ____ Not for Profit

                           ____ Service   ____ Public Sector

Organization Size: ____ 0–100   ____ 1000–5000

                           ____ 101–500   ____ 5001–10,000

                           ____ 501–1000   ____ Over 10,000

Your Title: _____M ____ F

Years in HR field: ____ 0–1   ____ 6–10

                        ____ 2–3   ____ Over 10

                        ____ 4–5

Ethnicity: ____ Caucasian   ____ Native American

                           ____ African American ____ Hispanic

                           ____ Asian   ____ East Indian

                    Other:_____

Age: ____ 30 or younger   ____ 51–60

                           ____ 31–40   ____ 60 or older

                           ____ 41–50

Part II—Scenarios

In the space provided, please respond to how you would handle the situation described if you encountered it in your organization. Feel free to use the back of the page if you need additional space.

Scenario #1

A highly productive manager in your organization, who was born and raised in the Middle East, finds a reason to reject all females recommended by Human Resources for professional or technical positions in his department. The manager is the CEO's son-in-law. What, if anything, should Human Resources do about this situation?

_____

_____

_____

_____

_____

_____

_____

_____

_____

_____

SCENARIO #2

A first-line supervisor within the organization has tested positive for HIV. He has advised Human Resources of this fact and that he intends to become a vocal community activist for gay rights. He indicated that he does not plan to disclose his diagnosis with coworkers. Who should Human Resources advise within the organization about this employee's illness and activist plans?

_____

_____

_____

_____

_____

_____

_____

_____

_____

Scenario #3

It is time for your organization to negotiate with the union for a new collective bargaining agreement. The union negotiator has requested information about potential mergers or sales of company divisions in preparation for negotiations. You have heard a rumor that a large company is interested in a merger or even acquisition of your company. Should you explore this rumor and disclose what you discover to the union negotiator?

_____

_____

_____

_____

_____

_____

_____

_____

_____

_____

Scenario #4

Robotics technology has resulted in a robot that can perform a dangerous, skilled labor job within the company. The CEO has indicated that she wants to immediately fire the employees who are currently performing this function and purchase the new technology. Should Human Resources start drawing up the paperwork to terminate these employees or take other steps?

_____

_____

_____

_____

_____

_____

_____

_____

Scenario #5

Recruiting for all positions within your organization has become very challenging. You are tempted when you are interviewing to assure potential employees that your company is financially stable, with little fluctuation in staffing and no organizational changes planned that will affect job descriptions. This may or may not be the case, because the company has experienced many changes in leadership and policies over the past 2 years. However, you have no current knowledge of instability or projected changes. What is your obligation to potential employees?

_____

_____

_____

_____

_____

_____

_____

_____

_____

_____

Scenario #6

Several employees within your organization have received permission to telecommute. Their managers are concerned that productivity may suffer because employees will not have direct supervision when they are working at home. Should you recommend technology that monitors log-in and log-out times, keystrokes, and sites they access on the Internet during work hours?

_____

_____

_____

_____

_____

_____

_____

_____

Scenario #7

Your organization has formed self-directed work teams that have a great deal of input into hiring and termination decisions, as well as rotation of team members across the organization. You have heard rumors in the lunchroom that two of the teams are experiencing internal conflict and are making recommendations based on personal likes and dislikes as opposed to peoples' skills. Should Human Resources intervene?

_____

_____

_____

_____

_____

_____

_____

_____

_____

_____

Thank you for taking time to complete this survey!

Appendix B

Examples of
Codes of Ethics

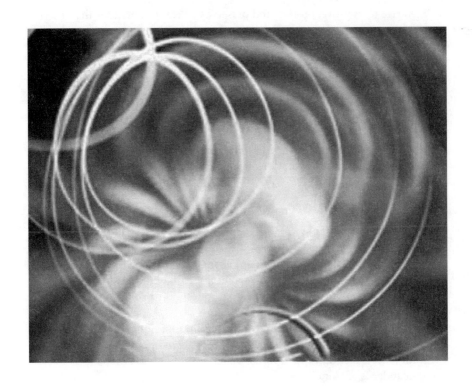

CDS Engineers

Ethics Guidelines

The credibility of our firm is dependent upon our striving to adhere to ethical standards. We believe that the following ideals are guidelines that will allow CDS Associates, Inc. to remain a vital and successful organization:

- Practice the virtue of treating others as we want to be treated
- Respect each individual's rights, property, and ideas
- Recognize and respect the value, dignity, and diverse individuality of all people in internal and external working relationships
- Be forthright, honest, and trustworthy in all business practices throughout every level of the organization
- Exercise sound judgment and avoid conflicts of interest when considering any activity that would compromise our working relationships with others
- Honor the confidentiality and sensitive nature of the various types of work performed by our firm
- Strive to improve, protect, and preserve our environment for the enhancement of neighborhoods and communities
- Expect that others who conduct business with our firm will strive to maintain the same ethical standards

Our commitment to a high standard of ethics and integrity reflects the value system established by CDS's founders. Our ethical standards are in response to a genuine, deep concern for doing what is right and fair in our activities and relationships.

Keeping our commitment and fulfilling the expectations that CDS Associates, Inc. creates should always be our uncompromising standard.

Clopay Corporation

Code of Business Ethics

- Employees shall conduct their employment activities with the highest principles of honesty, integrity, truthfulness and honor. To this end, employees are to avoid not only impropriety, but also the appearance of impropriety.
- Employees have a legal, moral and ethical responsibility to report to the Company or the appropriate authorities known or suspected violations of law, regulations, or corporate policy, including the Company's Standards of Conduct.

- Employees shall not make, recommend, or cause to be taken any action known or believed to be in violation of any law, regulation or corporate policy.
- Employees shall not make, recommend or cause to be made any expenditure of funds, whether corporate or private, known or believed to be in violation of any law, regulation or corporate policy.
- Employees shall not use their position in employment to force, induce, coerce, harass or intimidate, or in any manner influence any person, including subordinates, to provide any favor, gift or benefit, whether financial or otherwise, to themselves or others.
- In business dealings with government entities, whether U.S. or foreign, employees shall not provide or offer to provide, any gratuity, favor or other benefit to governmental employees, or engage in any other activity which could improperly influence, or reasonably be interpreted as improperly influencing, their decisions or activities. All such activities with government agencies shall be conducted strictly on an arm's length, business basis.
- Employees representing the Company to third parties shall not allow themselves to be placed in a position in which an actual or apparent conflict of interest exists. Such conflict of interest may arise, or appear to arise, by reason of the employees' acceptance of gratuities, favors or other valuable benefits which could improperly influence or reasonably be interpreted as improperly influencing sound business decisions. All such activities shall be conducted strictly on arm arm's length, business basis.
- Employees will exercise great care in situations in which a preexisting personal relationship exists between an employee and an industry representative or Government employee or official of an agency with whom the Company has an existing or potential business relationship. In such situations, the employee shall immediately report the relationship to management and, pending further direction by the Company, the employee shall take no further action associated with the business in which the personal relationship exists. Where there is any doubt as to the propriety of the relationship, the employee shall report the relationship to management so as to avoid even the appearance of impropriety.
- Employees shall not engage in outside business activities, either directly or indirectly, with a customer, vendor, supplier or agent of the Company, or engage in business activities of the Company.
- Employees shall not use or disclose the Company's trade secrets, proprietary or confidential information, or any other confidential information gained in the performance of Company duties as a means for making private profit, gain or benefit.

Cintas

Principles and Philosophies

We are a company of strong principles and values. We expect our partners to be compatible with these principles and values. People whose principles and values are inconsistent or incompatible with ours will not be happy here. We advise them to go elsewhere. After all, the beliefs our people share are responsible for our success, and will have more to do with our future accomplishments than anything else. Some of the principles and philosophies we share are:

High Moral Standards   We have high moral standards at Cintas. Our partners maintain professional business-like relationships with each other and guard against any personal conduct that could be considered morally offensive by another partner. We do not tolerate any type of discrimination or sexual harassment.

Honesty and Integrity   We do not cheat our partners, customers, or suppliers. We give honest answers to our superiors and associates. We give an accurate accounting of ourselves with carefully documented records. We honor our commitments and keep our promises. If we make a mistake, we admit it. We don't pass it off or cover it up.

Drug-Free Environment   Our partners believe in a work environment free of alcohol and drugs. A proper business-like atmosphere cannot be maintained without prohibiting the influence, possession or consumption of these items on company premises.

Use of Inside Information   Our partners do not purchase or sell (directly or indirectly) the stock of our company or any other company, based upon any information which they received as a result of their employment with Cintas not generally available to the public.

We Believe in Strict Separation of Business and Personal Affairs   Our partners avoid any situation which would cast doubt on our ability to act with total objectivity with respect to the company's interest. We want to be above reproach on these issues. Our business decisions are expected to be free of competing interests.

Gifts and Entertainment   We do not accept gifts or business favors. Normal business lunches are permitted. Dinners, entertainment, and trips may be accepted only when they have a definite business purpose and are approved by your supervisor. We do not want to do anything that would place us in a compromising position or cause us to lose our objectivity. We encourage professional relationships with our suppliers, and expect our suppliers to understand, respect, and cooperate with this policy.

Mutual Trust and Teamwork   Everyone starting a career at Cintas has our complete trust. They do not have to earn it. We believe our partners want to contribute; want the assurance their work is important; and want the opportunity to improve themselves in a successful organization. We work together and perform well as a team for our mutual interest of security, opportunity, personal reward and job satisfaction.

Confidentiality   Our partners recognize and protect the confidentiality of any information concerning the company, its business plans, personnel matters, new business efforts, customers, accounting and financial matters.

Self-Expression   While our basic beliefs and values are not subject to debate, our partners have the right to express their views—even opposing views when necessary. At Cintas we respect one another's opinions, even if they may differ from our own. We maintain a listening environment, and even when we disagree, we maintain respect.

Glossary

A

Acquired Immune Deficiency Syndrome (AIDS) A condition in which the body's defenses against some illnesses are broken down.

Acquisition One company acquires the stock of another company.

African American A person whose origin is any of the original black racial groups of Africa.

Age Discrimination in Employment Act (ADEA) A federal law passed in 1967 and amended in 1975 that prohibits discrimination in employment based on age for people age 40 or older.

Americans With Disabilities Act (ADA) A federal law passed in 1990 that prohibits discrimination in employment based on disability.

Asian A person whose origin is any of the original people in the Far East, Southeast Asia, Indian subcontinent, or Pacific Islands, including China, Japan, Korea, Philippine Islands, and Samoa.

B

Baby boomer The generation born between the years 1946–1964.

C

Caucasian A person whose origin is any of the original people of Europe, North Africa, or the Middle East.

Civil Rights Act A federal law passed in 1964 and amended in 1991 that prohibits discrimination in employment based on age, race, sex, religion, or national origin.

D

Decentralization Transfer of decision-making authority from a central focal point to dispersed division or department heads.

E

Ethnicity One's racial or cultural affiliation and heritage

Eurocentric A worldview related to or in support of a European, Caucasian heritage.

F

Fair Labor Standards Act (FLSA)
A federal law enforced by the
Department of Labor that was
passed in 1938 to establish a
minimum wage and overtime pay
obligation for over 40 hours
worked during one week.

**Family and Medical Leave Act
(FMLA)**   A federal law passed in
1993 that directs employers to
provide up to 12 weeks of paid or
unpaid leave during a 12-month
period to covered employees for
the birth of a child; placement of
a child for adoption or foster care;
caring for a spouse, child, or
parent with a serious health
condition; or the serious health
condition of the employee.

G

Gay rights   A homosexual man or
woman's rights such as
employment, worship, privacy,
and public safety.

Generation X   The generation born
between the years 1965–1976; also
referred to as "Baby Busters."

Generation Y   The generation born
between the years 1977–1985; also
referred to as "Generation Next."

Good faith bargaining
Negotiations in a union
environment in which both
parties attempt to reach a
satisfactory solution for all
involved stakeholders.

H

Hispanic   A person whose ethnic
heritage is Mexican, Puerto Rican,
Cuban, Central or South
American, or other Spanish
culture.

**Human Immunodeficiency Virus
(HIV)**   A virus that gradually
multiplies within the body and
eventually destroys the body's
ability to fight off illnesses.

Human Resource practitioner
A professional in a profit or
nonprofit organization who
actively practices in the Human
Resource Management field in
areas such as compensation,
training and development, and
employee relations.

L

Layoff   A temporary, involuntary
termination of one or more
positions, usually for an indefinite
time period.

M

Merger   Two companies combine
by exchanging stock.

N

**National Labor Relations Act
(NLRA)**   A federal law passed
in 1935 that guarantees workers
the right to join unions without
fear of management reprisal
and that prohibits employers
from committing unfair labor
practices.

**National Labor Relations Board
(NLRB)**   An independent federal
agency created in 1935 to enforce
the National Labor Relations Act.

Negotiations   Discussions between
union and management
representatives to settle matters
laid forth in the organization's
bargaining agreement.

O

Outplacement   A service provided for employees involved in layoffs or downsizing that provides assistance in the transition process, such as resume writing.

P

Prima facie   Latin term for "on its face"; superficial.

R

Radio babies   People born between 1930–1945; term refers to the fact that this generation listened to the radio for entertainment.

Relativism   The belief that no right or wrong exists out of context; each decision's ethical viability is relative to the environment surrounding that decision.

Robotics   Technology that enables rote, mundane tasks to be performed by machinery rather than by manual labor.

S

Securities and Exchange Commission (SEC)   A federal agency whose mission is to protect investors and maintain the integrity of the securities market.

Self-directed teams   Teams organized around function or across functions that make decisions about hiring and selection, work assignments, and re-assignment autonomously, with management guidance.

Strategic planning   Setting long-term objectives and goals that will assist the organization to achieve its Mission and Vision.

T

Telecommuting   Employees who have the option of completing all or a portion of their work off-site, typically in a home office.

Index

An italic *t* next to a page number (e.g., 177*t*) identifies information that appears in a table.

A

Abdicating responsibility, 8
Acquisitions. *See* Rumor exploration case
      study
African Americans
   empathy with discrimination victims, 22,
      23, 53
   employee replacement responses,
      100–102*t*, 102
   HIV-infected supervisor responses,
      58–61*t*, 61, 62
   recruiter honesty responses, 121–22*t*, 122,
      123
   rumor exploration responses, 86–87*t*, 87
   self-directed teams responses, 158–61*t*, 161
   sex discrimination responses, 17–21*t*, 22,
      23, 24
   telecommuter monitoring responses,
      137–38*t*, 139
Age level
   employee replacement responses, 106–7*t*,
      108
   HIV-infected supervisor responses,
      69–71*t*, 72, 81
   recruiter honesty responses, 126–27
   rumor exploration responses, 90–91
   self-directed teams responses, 164–67*t*, 167
   sex discrimination responses, 31–35*t*,
      39–40
   telecommuter monitoring responses,
      144–45*t*, 146
AIDS, 56. *See also* HIV-infected supervisor
      case study
Asians
   employee replacement responses,
      100–102*t*, 102, 103, 104
   HIV-infected supervisor responses,
      58–61*t*, 61, 62
   recruiter honesty responses, 121–22*t*, 122,
      123
   rumor exploration responses, 86–87*t*, 87
   self-directed teams responses, 158–61*t*, 161
   sex discrimination responses, 17–21*t*,
      22–23, 24
   telecommuter monitoring responses,
      137–38*t*, 138
Authority test, 10

B

Baby Boomers, 127, 167
Blame, shifting, 8
Books on ethics, 4
"Butterflies" test, 10

C

Caucasians
   employee replacement responses,
      100–102*t*, 103
   HIV-infected supervisor responses,
      58–61*t*, 61
   privacy concerns, 61
   recruiter honesty responses, 121–22*t*, 123
   rumor exploration responses, 86–87*t*, 87
   self-directed teams responses, 158–61*t*, 162
   sex discrimination responses, 17–21*t*, 22,
      23–24
   telecommuter monitoring responses,
      137–38*t*, 139
CDS Engineers code of ethics, 192
Centralized decision making, 113

Chief executive officers
approaching, by age and experience, 33*t*, 40
approaching, by gender, 29–30
approaching, by race and ethnicity, 16, 20*t*, 22
view of relation to manager, by age and experience, 31*t*, 40
view of relation to manager, by gender, 24–25*t*, 29
view of relation to manager, by organization size and type, 41*t*, 45–46*t*, 50, 51
view of relation to manager, by race and ethnicity, 14, 18*t*, 22
Cintas code of ethics, 194–95
Clopay Corp. code of ethics, 192–93
Coaching, 53, 155
Codes of ethics, 179, 181, 192–95
Communications, open, 181
Core values, 6, 178–79, 181–82
Counseling (HIV/AIDS)
author's opinion, 58
views by age level, 71*t*
views by experience level, 68–69*t*
views by gender, 64*t*
views by organization type, 75*t*
views by race and ethnicity, 61*t*
Cross-functional teams. *See* Self-directed teams case study
Cultural awareness, 15–16, 19*t*, 21*t*, 52

D

Decentralized decision making, 113
Discrimination. *See* Sex discrimination case study
Dishonest recruiting. *See* Recruiter honesty case study
Diversity training, 15–16, 19*t*, 23, 33*t*

E

Education, ongoing, 181–82. *See also* Training
Electronic monitoring systems, 134–35
Employee replacement case study
overall survey responses, 99–100, 116–17
overview, 98–99
responses by age level, 106–7*t*, 108
responses by experience level, 104–6*t*
responses by gender, 109–10*t*, 110–11
responses by organization size, 113–15*t*, 115–16

responses by organization type, 111–12*t*, 112–13
responses by race and ethnicity, 100–102*t*, 102–4
Ethical organizations
basic requirements, 6–8, 178–82
Human Resources role, 182–83
signs of weakness, 8–9
tests for individuals, 9–10
Ethics Resource Center Web site, 180
Ethics tests for individuals, 9–10
Ethnicity. *See* Race and ethnicity
Eurocentric perspective, 16
Expectations, ethical, 180
Experience level
employee replacement responses, 104–6*t*
HIV-infected supervisor responses, 65–69*t*
recruiter honesty responses, 125*t*, 127
rumor exploration responses, 89*t*, 90
self-directed teams responses, 162–64*t*, 167
sex discrimination responses, 35–39*t*, 39–40
telecommuter monitoring responses, 142–44*t*, 146

G

Gay rights activism
age level differences, 71*t*, 72
overall survey responses, 57–58, 81
responses by experience level, 68*t*
responses by gender, 64*t*, 65
responses by race and ethnicity, 60*t*, 62
Gender
employee replacement responses, 109–10*t*, 110–11
HIV-infected supervisor responses, 62–64*t*, 65, 81
rumor exploration responses, 87–88
self-directed teams responses, 155–57*t*, 157–58
sex discrimination responses, 24–28*t*, 28–30
telecommuter monitoring responses, 139–41*t*, 141–42
Generation Xers
concern for company image, 40, 108
desire to understand role, 121
reasons for joining organizations, 127
Generation Yers, 72, 127
Gilligan, Carol, 124
Good faith bargaining, 84–85, 86. *See also* Rumor exploration case study

H

Hierarchies, gender differences, 158
Hiring discrimination. *See* Sex discrimination case study
Hispanics
    employee replacement responses, 100–102*t*, 102, 103, 104
    HIV-infected supervisor responses, 58–61*t*, 61, 62
    recruiter honesty responses, 121–22*t*, 122
    rumor exploration responses, 86–87*t*, 87
    self-directed teams responses, 158–61*t*, 161, 162
    sex discrimination responses, 17–21*t*, 23, 24
    telecommuter monitoring responses, 137–38*t*, 138–39
HIV-infected supervisor case study
    overall survey responses, 56–58
    overview, 56
    responses by age level, 69–71*t*, 72, 81
    responses by experience level, 65–69*t*, 81
    responses by gender, 62–64*t*, 65, 81
    responses by organization size, 76–79*t*, 79–80
    responses by organization type, 73–75*t*, 75–76, 81
    responses by race and ethnicity, 58–61*t*, 61–62, 81
Honesty in recruiting. *See* Recruiter honesty case study
Human Resources
    ethics role, 182–83
    status and organization size, 51
    strategic planning role, 86, 95, 103, 116
    visibility, 181

I

Individual liability, 51
Innovation, trust and, 7
Internet Manager software, 134
Investigator software, 135

J

Japanese business culture, 22, 87
Job replacement. *See* Employee replacement case study
Johnson & Johnson, 6

K

Kohlberg, Lawrence, 9

L

Large organizations. *See* Organization size
Layoffs (robotics case study)
    overall survey responses, 100
    responses by age level, 107*t*
    responses by experience level, 106*t*
    responses by gender, 110*t*
    responses by organization size, 115*t*
    responses by organization type, 112*t*
    responses by race and ethnicity, 102*t*
Leaders as role models, 179–80
Litigation threats, 25*t*, 29
Lockheed Martin, 182

M

Manufacturing organizations
    employee replacement responses, 111–12*t*, 113
    HIV-infected supervisor responses, 73–75*t*, 76
    recruiter honesty responses, 128*t*, 129
    rumor exploration responses, 91–92*t*, 92
    self-directed teams responses, 168–70*t*, 170
    sex discrimination responses, 41–45*t*, 51
    telecommuter monitoring responses, 147–48*t*, 148
McMurray Publishing Company, 182
Mediocrity, 9
Men
    employee replacement responses, 109–10*t*, 110–11
    HIV-infected supervisor responses, 62–64*t*, 65
    recruiter honesty responses, 123–24*t*, 124
    rumor exploration responses, 87–88
    self-directed teams responses, 155–57*t*, 157–58
    sex discrimination responses, 24–28*t*, 28–30
    telecommuter monitoring responses, 139–41*t*, 141–42
Mergers. *See* Rumor exploration case study
Mistakes, Asian cultural view, 122
Mutual trust, 6–8, 179–80

N

National Business Ethics Survey, 180, 181
National Labor Relations Act (NLRA), 84
Not-for-profit organizations
    employee replacement responses, 111–12*t*
    HIV-infected supervisor responses, 73–75*t*, 75, 76

recruiter honesty responses, 128*t*, 129
rumor exploration responses, 91–92*t*,
    92–93
self-directed teams responses, 168–70*t*
sex discrimination responses, 41–45*t*, 50
telecommuter monitoring responses,
    147–48*t*, 149

O

Off-site workers. *See* Telecommuter
    monitoring case study
Ongoing education, 181–82
Open communications, 181
Organizations, ethical. *See* Ethical
    organizations
Organization size
    employee replacement responses, 113–15*t*,
        115–16
    HIV-infected supervisor responses,
        76–79*t*, 79–80
    recruiter honesty responses, 129–30*t*,
        130–31
    rumor exploration responses, 93*t*, 94
    self-directed teams responses, 171–73*t*,
        173–74
    sex discrimination responses, 45–50*t*,
        51–53
    telecommuter monitoring responses,
        149–51*t*, 151
Organization type
    employee replacement responses, 111–12*t*,
        112–13
    HIV-infected supervisor responses,
        73–75*t*, 75–76, 81
    rumor exploration responses, 91–92*t*,
        92–93
    self-directed teams responses, 168–70*t*,
        170–71
    sex discrimination responses, 41–45*t*,
        50–51
    telecommuter monitoring responses,
        147–48*t*, 148–49
Outplacement (robotics case study)
    overall survey responses, 100
    responses by age level, 107*t*
    responses by experience level, 105*t*
    responses by gender, 109*t*, 110–11
    responses by organization size, 114*t*, 116
    responses by organization type, 112*t*
    responses by race and ethnicity, 101*t*, 103
Overpromising, 8–9

P

Phase-in of robotics
    overall survey responses, 99–100
    responses by age level, 106*t*, 108
    responses by experience level, 104*t*
    responses by gender, 109*t*
    responses by organization size, 114*t*, 115
    responses by organization type, 111*t*
    responses by race and ethnicity, 101*t*, 103
Power distance, 102
Prima facie discrimination
    overall survey responses, 15
    responses by age and experience, 32*t*, 40
    responses by gender, 25*t*, 29
    responses by organization type and size,
        42*t*, 46*t*, 51, 52
    responses by race and ethnicity, 18*t*, 23–24
Privacy rights. *See* HIV-infected supervisor
    case study; Telecommuter
    monitoring case study
Productivity. *See* Telecommuter monitoring
    case study
Public relations. *See* Employee replacement
    case study
Public scrutiny test, 10
Public sector organizations
    employee replacement responses, 111–12*t*,
        112–13
    HIV-infected supervisor responses,
        73–75*t*, 76
    recruiter honesty responses, 128–29, 128*t*
    rumor exploration responses, 91–92*t*, 92
    self-directed teams responses, 168–70*t*
    sex discrimination responses, 41–45*t*, 50
    telecommuter monitoring responses,
        147–48*t*, 149

R

Race and ethnicity
    employee replacement responses,
        100–102*t*, 102–4
    HIV-infected supervisor responses,
        58–61*t*, 61–62, 81
    recruiter honesty responses, 121–23
    rumor exploration responses, 86–87*t*, 87
    self-directed teams responses, 158–61*t*,
        161–62
    sex discrimination responses, 17–21*t*,
        22–24
    telecommuter monitoring responses,
        137–38*t*, 138–39

Radio babies, 127
Recruiter honesty case study
    overall survey responses, 120–21, 131
    overview, 120
    responses by age and experience, 125–26t,
        126–27
    responses by gender, 123–24t, 124
    responses by organization size, 129–30t,
        130–31
    responses by organization type,
        128–29, 128t
    responses by race and ethnicity, 121–23
Respect, 6–8, 179–80
Respondent data, 11t
Responsibility, abdicating, 8
Retraining and reassignment
    overall survey responses, 99, 116
    responses by age level, 106t
    responses by experience level, 104t
    responses by gender, 109t
    responses by organization size, 114t, 115
    responses by organization type, 111t
    responses by race and ethnicity, 100t, 102
Robotics, 3, 98. See also Employee replacement
    case study
Role models, 179–80
Rumor exploration case study
    overall survey responses, 85–86
    overview, 84–85
    responses by age and experience, 89–90t,
        90–91
    responses by gender, 87–88
    responses by organization size, 93t, 94
    responses by organization type, 91–92t,
        92–93
    responses by race and ethnicity, 86–87t, 87
Rumors. See Rumor exploration case study;
    Self-directed teams case study

S

Scapegoating, 8
Self-directed teams case study
    overall survey responses, 154–55, 174–75
    overview, 154
    responses by age and experience, 162–67t,
        167
    responses by gender, 155–57t, 157–58
    responses by organization size, 171–73t,
        173–74
    responses by organization type, 168–70t,
        170–71
    responses by race and ethnicity, 158–61t,
        161–62

Self-directed work teams, challenges, 3–4, 154
Service organizations
    employee replacement responses, 111–12t,
        112, 113
    HIV-infected supervisor responses,
        73–75t, 76
    recruiter honesty responses, 128–29
    rumor exploration responses, 91–92t, 92
    self-directed teams responses, 168–70t,
        170–71
    sex discrimination responses, 41–45t, 51
    telecommuter monitoring responses,
        147–48t, 148–49
Sex discrimination case study
    overall survey responses, 14–17
    overview, 14
    responses by age and experience, 30–39t,
        39–40
    responses by gender, 24–28t, 28–30
    responses by organization size, 45–50t,
        51–53
    responses by organization type, 41–45t,
        50–51
    responses by race and ethnicity, 17–21t,
        22–24
Small organizations. See Organization size
Society for Human Resource Management
    Web site, 15, 51, 182
Super Scout software, 135
Surveillance. See Telecommuter monitoring
    case study
Survey respondent profile, 11t
Survivor in Africa, 174–75
Swim With the Dolphins, 29, 30

T

Teams. See Self-directed teams case study
Telecommuter monitoring case study
    overall survey responses, 136–37, 152
    overview, 134–35
    responses by age and experience, 142–45t
    responses by gender, 139–41t, 141–42
    responses by organization size,
        149–51t, 151
    responses by organization type, 147–48t,
        148–49
    responses by race and ethnicity, 137–38t,
        138–39
Telecommuters, expectations for, 180
Tests, ethics, 9–10
Toyota, 6

Training. *See also* Retraining and reassignment
 in core values, 6
 diversity, 15–16, 19*t*, 23
 hiring and selection, 16, 158, 167
Trust, 6–8, 179–80. *See also* Telecommuter
 monitoring case study
Truthfulness in recruiting. *See* Recruiter
 honesty case study
Turf guarding, 9
Tylenol scare, 6

U

Underachieving, 9
Unions. *See also* Rumor exploration case study
 challenges, 3
 legal bargaining position, 84–85
 membership by gender, 87

V

Values, 6, 178–79, 181–82

W

Web sites
 AIDS, 56
 Asian business culture, 22, 23
 ethics, 4
 Ethics Resource Center, 180
 gender differences, 124
 Kohlberg books, 9
 robotics, 98
 Society for Human Resource
  Management, 15, 51, 182
Women
 employee replacement responses, 109–10*t*,
  110–11
 HIV-infected supervisor responses,
  62–64*t*, 65
 recruiter honesty responses, 123–24*t*, 124
 rumor exploration responses, 87–88
 self-directed teams responses, 155–57*t*, 158
 sex discrimination responses, 24–28*t*,
  28–30
 telecommuter monitoring responses,
  139–41*t*, 141–42